BETWEEN EARTH AND HEAVEN

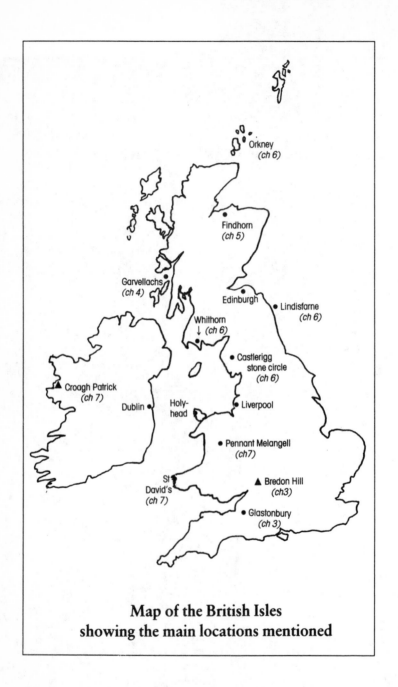

**Map of the British Isles
showing the main locations mentioned**

Orkney
(ch 6)

Findhorn
(ch 5)

Garvellachs
(ch 4)

Edinburgh

Lindisfarne
(ch 6)

Whithorn
↓ (ch 6)

Castlerigg
stone circle
(ch 6)

Croagh Patrick
(ch 7)

Dublin

Holy-
head

Liverpool

Pennant Melangell
(ch7)

St
David's
(ch 7)

▲ Bredon Hill
(ch3)

Glastonbury
(ch 3)

Between Earth and Heaven

A Journey into Sacred Space

By Chris Peck

ARTHUR JAMES

BERKHAMSTED

First published in 1997 by

ARTHUR JAMES LTD
70 Cross Oak Road
Berkhamsted
Hertfordshire HP4 3HZ

A catalogue record for this book is available
from the British Library.

ISBN 0 85305 366 9

Typeset in Sabon by Watermark
Cromer NR27 9HL

Printed in Great Britain by
The Ipswich Book Company

For Alison
whose courageous way of facing death from cancer
has inspired me on my journey

Contents

List of Maps

Acknowledgements

This book would not have been possible without the support and encouragement of Sirpa, Antony and Nina. Lavinia Byrne first encouraged me to write it and recommended me to a publisher; Sister June and Brother Ramon became spiritual companions on the journey; Steve Cousens, Chris Powell, June and Sirpa read first drafts and gave wise advice; Sandra Wellington and Di Williams shouldered the work while I was travelling; Anne Winstanley patiently plouhed her way through dictaphone tapes; Mike Williams gave wise supervision for my master's dissertation; Lance Pierson offered detailed advice on negotiating a contract; Judith Longman enabled it to become a publishable book. The journey would not have been possible without the generous support of the Diocese of Liverpool and the book would not have seen the light of day without the staff at Arthur James. Finally, my father, Dennis Peck, ensured that I grew up in a household where writing was an everyday occurrence.

A journey . . . is at once outward and inward. It serves as a doorway to a new awareness. A larger experience of one's own self. An unconscious knowledge from a wise source generates a sense of fulfilment. It leads one into a state of silent enchantment which sends one away transformed and renewed.
Sharat Kumar[1]

Introduction

The world is charged with the grandeur of God.
Gerard Manley Hopkins[2]

*This is none other than the house of God; it is the
gateway of heaven.*
Genesis 28:17

Jacob was on the run when he came to the little shrine near
Luz. He had stolen his brother's birthright with a dirty trick.
His brother was furious and was out to kill him. Instead of
enjoying the fruit of his crime, here he was, a fugitive travelling alone, too afraid to seek hospitality in the nearby town.
We can picture him as he takes a stone from the ground to use
as a pillow, and imagine the feelings of guilt, fear, anger and
aching loneliness racing through him. As he lay on the hard
ground trying to protect himself from the cold of the night, it
was probably a long time before he finally dropped off into a
restless sleep disturbed by numerous dreams. But one dream
was different. It had a clarity about it which made it stand
out. He could remember every detail, every word spoken to
him. It took him totally by surprise because suddenly he was
taken into a different world, a world where the gap between
earth and heaven was bridged by a ladder with angels moving
freely up and down. Instead of being at the top of the ladder

God was standing beside him and speaking words, not of condemnation for his crime, but of blessing. No wonder that when Jacob wakes up the story-teller describes him as being 'awestruck'. At the moment when he would have felt most like shrinking from God, placed by deceit on the outskirts of society and humanity, at that moment he is met by God who lavishes him with blessings. It is no wonder that he says, 'This is none other than the house of God; it is the gateway of heaven.'[3] He has a need to mark this encounter, so he takes the stone on which he has been sleeping, sets it up as a sacred pillar and pours oil over it. And so the shrine of Bethel was established which was to be a major focus of worship for the people of Israel for hundreds of years, a sacred place.

In the summer of 1995 I had the opportunity to make a three-month journey as part of a sabbatical from my work as an adult educator with the Anglican church in Liverpool. I visited many such sacred sites, some like Stonehenge and Avebury consisting of stones, others with abbeys and churches, others natural sites and holy islands. It was a journey into sacred places but it became more than that. As I travelled around sacred sites I found myself making an interior journey into the sacred space inside. It was exhilarating and at times painful. Like Jacob, I felt very alone at moments. Like Jacob, I was forced to face aspects of myself which I would gladly have avoided. And like Jacob, I found myself being encountered by God in totally unexpected ways. I was blessed with many glimpses of heaven, glimpses which have come to alter the way I experience the earth and the world which makes up my daily life. Like Jacob, I feel that at some profound level I am a different person from the one who set out on the journey.

This is a personal account of that journey. I visited over a hundred sites in the British Isles. I went with underlying questions: 'What makes for "sacred space"? Are there particular

places which have the power to speak to us of God? Are there
clues in the revival of interest in the "sacred" in our society
for our churches?' I spent eight days in solitude on an
uninhabited island, and a week with the 'new age' community
at Findhorn. We live in a rapidly changing society. Alongside
rampant materialism we are seeing a renewal of interest in
spiritual and sacred matters. Much of this interest, however,
is happening outside the churches. Would I be able to find the
clues as to why this is?

The account is a reflective one. I used the opportunity to
gather material for a dissertation on 'God and Place' for a
Master's in Theology. That included getting a high proportion of replies to a questionnaire for church people on their
experience of God and place. While this book draws on that
material it is written for ordinary people and is not academic
in its approach. There are reflections woven into the account
of the journey, and the ninth chapter summarizes some of
the things I believe I learnt about God and place. It also
draws out implications for our churches. Those who are
looking for definitive answers to 'What makes for sacred
space?' will not find easy ones. In exploring this area I found
myself touching on the point where heaven and earth meet at
the heart of the mystery which gives life meaning. But I
believe that the account does offer some clues, some indica-
tions, and suggests ways forward for exploring this fascinating
subject.

I hope the book will whet your appetite for visiting sites
which have something of a sacredness and holiness about
them. I have been thrilled to discover so many wonderful sites
dotted around our islands. I only describe a selection of the
ones I went to. I was afraid I might get tired of visiting, and lose
a sense of the 'specialness' of places. Occasionally the pace did
feel relentless, but more often I discovered that time and again
I was awed by a sense of God mediated through particular

sites. Occasionally a site would turn out to be a disappointment but I was struck by how many of them spoke powerfully to me. Time and again I was filled with wonder by the beauty of the world we inhabit. My hope is that something of that deep sense of wonder comes through this account.

I also became aware of how personal sacred space can be. What one person experiences as being a 'sacred' site will not be the same for another. Even sites which are recognised by many as being 'sacred' are not experienced in that way by all. This was brought home forcefully to me as I was completing this book. I managed to get hold of a copy of a book called *In Search of Stones* by M Scott Peck,[4] which had just been published in America. In it he describes a journey visiting prehistoric and other sites. His experience of some sites was very different to mine. For example, he spent a short time on the Celtic island of Iona and felt there was nothing special about it. I am aware therefore that some people will look for favourite sites and find them not mentioned. Others will feel that I have not done justice to places which for them are deeply special.

It is also a personal account of an exploration undertaken by a forty-five-year-old man facing all the issues of mid-life about identity, meaning and purpose. I was unable to separate out the psychological journey from the physical one, nor would I have wanted to. Stepping outside the routine of everyday life not only shook up my experience of where God is to be found, but also my personal and family relationships, my relatedness to the Church and my experience of the masculine and feminine aspects of my psyche. The account is written from the perspective of someone with a Christian commitment, who works for the Church. But because it touches on the deep human things which affect all of us, whatever our life situation and belief, it will speak to anyone who has a sense of spiritual longing and a desire to experience the sacred.

The theme of a journey emerged naturally for me as being

the symbol around which to weave the account. It is the theme which makes most sense of my experience of my life and Christian faith to date. I grew up in a liberal home. My mother was a deeply spiritual person but not a committed Christian. Art was my father's religion. I went to Sunday School as a young child but did not have any Christian commitment until my teens, when I was converted in a conservative evangelical context which profoundly shaped my experience of the Christian faith. I gained a deep sense of Jesus as my personal saviour and a love for the Bible. Since then my life has taken me to a variety of places and a variety of contexts. In each of them I have found aspects of my beliefs questioned, but in the process discovered my faith and my sense of God being enriched. I have benefited from the charismatic, liberal, catholic, orthodox and radical traditions of the Church. The sense of God with which I started out on this particular bit of my journey owes something to all of them. I feel that my experience has been similar to that of the people of Israel, being led into event after event and discovering through them God revealed as being more wonderful than they had dreamed possible. Like the early Church, my experience has been of discovering that the good news of Jesus has wider implications than I at first realised. I feel as though I am being taken on a journey through life. At each step so far I have discovered that I can trust God in new situations because each time my sense of God is enlarged through my experience.

This is an account of a particularly dramatic step forward in my journey. Most of my life is extremely humdrum and ordinary, full of the business of making ends meet, coping with the demands of work and relationships, feeling that I barely have energy to cope day by day. The sabbatical gave me the opportunity to take the risk of stepping outside this everyday life. As I did so I experienced God meeting me in extraordinary ways. The effect, however, has been to enable me to discover God in the ordinary.

The sharing of this particular part of my journey is in the hope that it will re-stimulate your desire to enter as fully as possible into the particular journey of faith that you are on. I had a tremendous sense of privilege at being able to undertake such a journey, and therefore wanted to be able to share something of it with others. Like the person who goes on a pilgrimage and comes back with some token of where they have been to share with friends, I want to say 'This is what I have discovered'. You may want to read it simply as an account of someone else's life and journey. But I hope that reading it will in itself be a step on your journey and lead you to travel on more deeply into an experience of the God who goes before us towards the promised land.

Notes

1. in *Resurgence* Jan/Feb 1996, issue 174, p36
2. Poems and Prose of Gerard Manley Hopkins, selected by W H Gardner, Penguin 1953, p27
3. Genesis 28:17
4. *In Search of Stones*, M Scott Peck, Hyperion 1995

PART 1

Preparations for Travel

1

A Journey Takes Shape

*The Lord said to Abram 'Leave your own country,
your kin and go.'*
Genesis 12:1

Beginnings

When does a journey begin? Is it the moment that you shut
the front door behind you and set off; or the moment that you
begin to pack; or that delicious moment when you begin to
conceive the trip and dream of all the possibilities? Or does it
start further back, in the mists of the unconscious, before you
even know that the possibility exists? As I look back I can see
many starting points for my journey. But the moment that
stands out goes back several years to a particular night which
has remained etched on my memory.

It was a cold, frosty, February evening. I was on my way to
a mid-week communion at our local parish church, some five
minutes' walk from where we lived. As I stepped outside, I
felt immediately that it was a magical night. The sky was
clear, there was frost in the air, shapes stood out starkly
against the black sky. As I came over the brow of the hill leading down to the church hidden in the valley, I was brought to
a standstill by the sight of a single conifer silhouetted against
the moon. The moon was full, a perfect globe pinned to the

sky and filling the earth with an eerie, pure glow. It was as though I had never seen anything so beautiful. My heart was beating wildly, a surge of excitement swept through me. For a moment I was rooted to the spot, unable to take my eyes away from the beauty that was piercing me. And I had a deep, deep sense that it would be sinful, unforgivable, to go into a building on a night like that. Everything in my being, everything that seemed to me to speak of God, from God, was calling me to be outside, to praise, worship in the open air. And so instead of going to the service I turned away from the church, and walked the quiet streets, praising God, filled to the brim with an energy and a joy and an awe and a wonder, fearful of turning back, fearful of losing the magic of those minutes, wanting to stay within that sense of the presence of God filling the earth, baptising every paving stone, every tree, every gateway, every house, every nerve and fibre of my body as I walked.

I could not ignore or deny the power of that feeling of God in nature. But I was faced with a dilemma. I was a full-time church worker, a lay training officer with the Anglican Diocese of Southwark. I had been on my way to a communion service, which is the central act of Christian worship for those in my tradition. And I was experiencing a sense of God coming from outside, through the natural world, that was speaking more powerfully to me than anything I had experienced within church worship. Was this something alien, something to be avoided, something which would lead me away from Christian faith? Or was I, through that sense of God in nature, encountering something that the Christian Church has lost sight of? Had I touched on a whole dimension of worship missing from much of the Christian tradition that had become the focus not only of faith but also of my work and sense of being? Alongside the deep, lasting sense of joy I had experienced was a nagging guilt and an underlying question: Was I in some way betraying Christ? But also, half formed, was the question: Had the Church in some way been betraying me by appearing to deny access to a whole realm of experiencing God? I had to wait some years before the pieces began to come together.

It was some four years later, when I stood by the ruins of the abbey on the Celtic island of Lindisfarne, that that memory flooded back, and it seemed that this part of my journey had begun that night, so many moons before. I had moved from Southwark to take up the post of Director of Development for Mission with Liverpool Diocese, with my wife, Sirpa, a Finn, and our two children, Antony and Nina. Some years earlier I had discovered the benefit of spending a few days each year in retreat. In my teens I had been converted into a very protestant, evangelical expression of Christianity, where the idea of silence in prayer was very alien, so the idea of spending some days in total silence, including meals, seemed very strange at first. I discovered however that the experience stilled me in my depths and enabled me to be in tune with God and my life at a deeper level. I had gone to a Roman Catholic convent near Hindhead, and once I had overcome my fears had come to love the place and to value the discipline of staying with a passage of Scripture in total quiet for up to an hour, noting down everything that happened to me as I did so. When I moved up to Liverpool, I was keen to continue the practice. But where to go?

One day I was looking at a road atlas and my eye was led to Lindisfarne, Holy Island. Half-remembered images, pictures and a very brief visit to the castle made as a tourist many years earlier came flooding back. I had a deep inner desire to go there. I asked around and discovered there was a community on the island, with a cottage where people could make retreat. And so I set off in the car one October to make the journey. As I travelled up into Northumbria I found myself lost in wonder at the beauty of the countryside round Rothbury, the car winding up and down thickly wooded hills which were beginning to display their autumn colours of red, gold, orange and deep browns. I felt my heart racing as I came nearer and nearer to the island. Strangely, the nearer I got the more my heart sank. The coast was flat, dull, uninspiring. It seemed bleak, unfriendly, unwelcoming. The most obvious feature across the sea was an ugly watertower, surrounded by what looked from a distance like poky little houses. There were no cliffs or outstanding natural features. I wondered what I had come to.

My heart continued to sink as I turned into the small cul de sac where the cottage was. It felt cold. An initial walk around did something to alleviate my feelings but I was still left with a sense of disappointment. There were a few houses, mostly with little character, and a few shops, mostly full of touristy bits and pieces. By the shore I began to feel something of the atmosphere of the place as I looked over to tiny Cuthbert's isle which is cut off by the tide twice a day, under the shadow of the parish church, itself somewhat squat and square. Further round I climbed up a hillock from where I could look over the Abbey ruins and across to the castle, which seems to grow out of the rock which itself appears to grow out of the bed of the island. However, I still felt very flat when I arrived back at my little room and wondered why I had come.

In time, I grew to love Lindisfarne, perhaps more than any other place I have visited. I grew to love the ebb and flow of the life on the island – the high tide of people when the sea tide is low and the island is accessible, followed by the silence and solitary nature of the high tide when the island is cut off from the mainland, the people have gone, and the island reclaims itself. I grew to love the atmosphere of the area by the ruined Abbey and Cuthbert's island. I would stand, just soaking up the atmosphere while time stood still. I grew to love the view across the bay to the rock and the castle. I grew to love the walk around the coast to the far side where very few people penetrated, and seals were always to be seen bobbing up and down in the water. I grew to love the feel of the tough, rough grass under my feet, the wind on my cheeks, the contrast of stones and sand, and all around the sea, with its constantly changing moods and taste of salt on the lips.

In the mornings I would meditate, pray, write. In the afternoons I would walk, soak in the island, whatever the weather, whatever its moods. One day I left to explore Berwick-on-Tweed. It was a mistake. The island was where I wanted to be. The memory which stands out for me is one of the night before I was due to leave. It was a wild, stormy night, with the wind whipping up the waves in a frenzy of turbulence. I went out and stood on the hillock. I could hardly breathe because the wind snatched the air away before I had time to fill my lungs. I could barely stand and was afraid I might be carried off into the air. I suddenly felt the power of a transcendent, creator God, in the light of whom all our plans and schemes and beliefs and institutions felt puny and weak and vulnerable. The whole of the civilisation that we have built up and glory in, with all its technology, seemed as nothing in the face of the power of these elements. I felt no fear but only awe. And I experienced a sense that this reality I was experiencing at this moment was deeper and more fundamental than all the rest.

And it was through the first visit to Lindisfarne that I discovered the Celtic Christian tradition – a tradition that hit me like a breath of fresh air, blowing through much of the mustiness of the Christianity that I had been formed through. I discovered a people who were in touch with nature and its rhythms and who experienced them as the rhythm of God. I discovered a people for whom God was not simply out there or up there, nor contained within the hearts of his chosen people, but was to be experienced and encountered in every aspect of life and matter – in the sea and land, in the rocks and stones, in the animals and birds, in every person met. I discovered Christian leaders whose deep desire to be in touch with that God led them to do crazy things like praying throughout the night up to their chest in water but allowing themselves to be dried by the otters in the morning. I discovered a tradition of a people on the move, restlessly thrusting out, beyond, into new territories, for whom community life was the place from which to go out into the unknown, not a resting place in which to retreat from the world outside. I discovered a people for whom the transcendent was immanent, who lived in a world occupied by angels and spiritual beings as well as humans, where departed saints were present to them and accompanying them on their journey. I discovered a people for whom rhythm, poetry, imagery and symbol were natural modes of communication, who gloried in God in the natural rhythm of everyday life, of getting up, working, sleeping. I discovered a people who had a deep sense of God as Trinity – Father, Son and Holy Spirit, three in one and one in three – as the one who daily protected them against evil. And for the first time in my life I felt that a whole part of me, a deep part of my experience of God, had a place, a home, within the Christian tradition.

Discovering Celtic Christianity was a deeply healing experience for me because it began the process of integrating two parts of myself which up until then had been held apart. There was the 'good Christian' part, the part of me that responded to the call of Christ as a teenager, that invited Christ into my life and sought to follow him in all I did and was; the part that faithfully read my Bible, prayed every day and felt guilty when I didn't; the part that drew me to take regular communion, share in weekly Christian worship, to study theology, to live and work in a Christian community, to go on to work 'full time' for the Church as an adult educator and trainer; the part that experienced constant renewal and enrichment through encountering different Christian traditions and being touched by the charismatic movement, the radical thinking and actions of groups like the Sojourners community, the deeply committed 'middle of the road' Anglicans, Anglo-Catholic spirituality and worship, informal house groups and African revivalist faith during two years spent in Kenya.

And alongside that, at a deeper level, often unacknowledged, there was another part of me. A part that responds to God in nature, a part that has deep intense experiences of God when I am on my own outside in the hills and the countryside that feel sexual in their intensity, the part of me that feels moved by the sight of a full moon at a level that is beyond words and deeper than any of my experience of God in Christian worship, the part of me that needs to get out into the country every so often to experience a re-energising and renewing in the depths of my being, something which can find expression in simply standing with my hand on a tree in silent communion, something which feels at times dangerously like nature worship, paganism, something to be kept secret and separate from the religious part of me. It was a whole realm of experience that I felt traditional Christianity did not accept or understand, and so was a part of me that was unnourished by my experience of church.

Suddenly I had discovered in Celtic Christianity a whole stream within my own Christian tradition that affirmed, celebrated, owned, acknowledged that part of me which was drawn into worship through nature that the evangelical, Anglican Christianity, into which I had been converted and with which I continued to struggle, seemed to find little place for.

Background

The experience that frosty February evening was a starting place for me because it focused something so powerfully that I could not deny its reality. It focused something which for me had always been a part of my experience, sometimes alive, sometimes dormant, but always there. And that something seemed to be associated not just with nature in general, not any nature anywhere, but with particular places, particular experiences. As I discovered a Christian tradition in which there was a deep awareness of God being present in particular places, and reflected back on my experience, I became aware of how special places have renewed me at a deep level of being.

I grew up on a farm in the Cotswolds. Although my father sold the farm soon after I was born, he kept the spacious Cotswold stone farm house with its view over miles of rolling hills and a wood sheltering it on two sides. My early childhood was very lonely. My mother had grown up in upper class New York society and had very firm ideas about 'unsuitable children' and the evils of dirt, so I was not allowed to play with the other children on the farm. My brother and sister were both older and away at school, so many hours were spent on my own in the woods, climbing trees, damming streams and playing. I remember a certain oak tree, set in a little glade, with deep lines running down its bark, which drew me back again and again; also a little bridge over a stream at the bottom of the big field out of sight of the house; and an avenue of tall, majestic beech trees.

When I was five the money ran out and we moved to live in a primitive bungalow set under the lee of Carn Llidi, overlooking St David's Head in Wales. There were views from the veranda across the moorland out to sea with Ramsay Island in the distance. Some of the rocks of Carn Llidi at the back of the house became very special for me, as did St David's Head itself, with the occasional seal bobbing up in the water and the flash of quartz in some of the stones.

I was sent to boarding school on the Malvern Hills. We spent many hours playing on the hillside but one place stands out in particular. Every third Sunday we used to walk to the British Camp, an ancient hill fort. Each time I found my imagination stirred and could see small, dark people defending themselves against marauders. It seemed as though there was a lingering presence in the place which had the power to break through the cans of drink and sweet papers and put me in touch with a people who were strangely connected with me, close to me, in a way that I found allowed me to feel emotions which the school was teaching me as a boy to be wary of and deny.

And it was at a certain place in the countryside that I had one of the deepest encounters with God that I have experienced. I was on a conference near Birmingham. During one of the breaks I went out into the formal gardens which had a fence bordering a rough meadow. Suddenly, it was as though the garden and all the landscape around me was my life, my world, my experience. I felt impelled to climb over the fence into the meadow. At the same time I felt very afraid. I was at home, safe, secure in the garden. I continued to pace around it, afraid to go too near the border, afraid of the wildness and wilderness on the other side, afraid of what it represented in terms of moving out of the security of my existence, the known, the familiar. And yet I could not resist the urge. Summoning up courage from inside, I approached the fence, hesitated, and then climbed over and jumped into the meadow. To my total astonishment I found myself in a world of beauty, variety, scents, colours and sounds. Wherever I looked there were wild flowers and a bewildering variety of different coloured grasses; there were butterflies flying –

yellow, brown, red, blue. There were birds that would fly up
out of the grass as I came near. Far from being in a rough wilderness I was in a world of beauty and variety, a world where
I felt more at home, more safe than in the 'security' of the
formal gardens, and I found my eyes filling with tears as I
realised that I had nearly missed the experience through my
need to stay in safety. It was so real that the only way I could
make sense of it was in terms of God appearing to me in a
special way at that moment, offering me a parable, calling me
to step out in the whole of my life, to discover him at the
borders, to be prepared to live on the edge and step over the
artificial barriers I was putting up, in order to discover the
richness and variety and wonder of the wilderness.

When I started working for the Church we moved to South
London and lived on the edge of suburbia. Every so often I
would take off in the car and explore different areas of
countryside. One day I found myself near a little village called
Findon and walked. Suddenly it was as though I was on holy
ground; there was something special about the place, particularly in the distance a small hill rising out of the plain with a
clump of trees on the top. The nearer I got, the more my heart
raced and the sense of specialness grew until I was standing
on the mound, under the trees. From that moment on it
became an important place to visit every so often, and I discovered that whenever I did so I became re-energised. I later
discovered that the place was Cissbury Ring, an ancient hill
fort.

We now live in Liverpool on the edge of a Victorian park.
It has woodland, lakes and bubbling streams. It leads on to
Otterspool with its miles of grassland and promenade along
the Mersey. Between them are Otterspool woods, an area of
ancient woodland, a dark, mysterious place which draws me
back time and again. And through the woods there is a bowl
of grass surrounded by high banks, some clear, some wooded.

From one of the banks you can look down on this grassy bowl and simultaneously across the width of the Mersey to the Welsh mountains. I cannot cycle near the spot without stopping and becoming still, experiencing that sense of deep renewal and re-energising.

Experiencing the sacred

Three other experiences stand out particularly for me. One was four years ago when one hot May bank holiday weekend I went camping with friends in the Lake District, together with our daughter Nina, then nine years old. We were on our way back from a long walk through the hills when we came on a stream running under a wooden bridge filled with rocks. As we looked up we could see it emerging from a gap in the hillside and catch a glimpse of a waterfall hidden in its recesses. Two of the others with more courage than I began to climb up, followed by Nina. Hesitantly, I followed and managed to scramble up the rocks. Suddenly I found myself in another, deeply mysterious world. Ferns and mosses clung to the sides of a deep cleft. Tiny trees clung perilously to the cliff walls. Looking up, I could just see shafts of sunlight filtering through. But the focus of my attention was the water – a constant stream pouring down with a thundering, continuous sound. From a distance I was already wet with the spray. At the base of the waterfall there was a swirling mass of white water where it plunged into the pool but the rest of the pool itself was perfectly still. Somehow, we could not be there and not acknowledge, not enter into its depths, but they were not to be entered into lightly. Quietly, we stripped off. One by one, we slipped gasping into the icy water and swam to the edge of the turbulence, feeling the power of the water from the heights and its constancy, never ceasing, never ending. The whole world around seemed to melt into one as we swam in awe. The next morning the others left for home and we had an extra day. I wasn't surprised when Nina said in a hushed voice, 'Can we go back to that place?' I didn't need to ask her what she meant, and I was only too ready to agree. A second visit can never be the same as that first moment when you realise that you are standing on holy ground, standing in a sacred place, but something of that magic was still there.

The second memory that stands out took place in the summer of 1993. We had gone to Ireland for a family holiday. We camped near Galloway, very near the sea. Near the campsite were some woods. One morning I was awoken very early by the sun. It was about 5.30 and I felt impelled to get up. I was unusually alert, awake and energised. It was almost as though I was being called to go out. I struggled to put my clothes on, trying not to wake Nina or Sirpa as I did so, and crept out. It was a glorious morning, very still and sunny, cold in the early morning air, but with a promise of warmth to come. I went through the small woods and turned to go down a track towards the sea. Suddenly, I stopped with my heart beating wildly. In the woods I could see a tiny clearing. The sun was filtering through the multi-layered leaves and shining directly into the clearing. In the middle of it, standing on its own, was a Celtic cross. I went in and felt an awe coming over me. The area around the cross was gravelled. It looked like a memorial but there was no writing. I had a deep sense of being on holy ground, of having been given a gift just through the experience of standing in that place. Time seemed to stand still.

Eventually, I tore myself away and continued on down towards the sea. I felt uplifted. There was a feel of magic in the air. I climbed on to a grassy field above some low cliffs and stood still, looking out to sea. My eye was caught by what looked like a group of seals. As they came nearer I realised that they were a school of porpoises or dolphins making their way up the bay. I watched them as they danced through the water until they disappeared out of sight. I turned slowly, about to walk on, and became aware of a fox a few yards away standing and watching me. I stared back. After a few moments he decided that I was of no further interest and ambled away. I walked back to the tent in a trancelike state. I felt that I had been lifted to see the world in a different way, that I was in a magical, holy place and that in the inter-connectedness I felt with the creation around me I was in touch with God in the depths of my body, that my whole being had been stilled by the experience. I felt a new sense of reverence and respect for the earth of which I am a part.

The following day I became aware as I walked of the amount of litter strewn around this quiet part of southern Ireland. I began to collect it. I could suddenly see the litter choking the earth, the earth not being able to breathe because of the cloak of litter muffling it. I was shocked at how quickly I collected a sackful of the stuff. Questions of the environment and its future suddenly became part of me, instead of being something 'out there'. It was as though there was a tiny bit of me that was feeling as the earth might be feeling. It was my first experience of the earth as a living, breathing entity, created by God but being suffocated by humankind. When I shared my experience of seeing the sea-creatures and the fox Nina was jealous of what she had missed, and asked me to take her the following day. The weather was different and we saw nothing.

Earlier that summer I had had a similar experience. I was attending a conference at Durham, a place I hadn't known before. I had gone into the Cathedral the previous day and found it full of hustle and bustle and business, and I hadn't stayed. The following morning I woke early and it was as though the morning was calling me out and I felt energised. Slipping quietly out, I made my way down the wooded hill to a little spring where the water was gushing out. Nearby a

starling stood and watched me, tilting its little head to one
side and staring with its beady eye. I carried on, and felt a
deep stillness coming over me. I crossed the river, and climbed
up into the woods, gazing at the huge trees and reaching out
to feel them, longing to be in contact with them. I stood by
one looking up in awe into its massive strength reaching up
towards the sky. I felt an aching longing inside to be for ever
part of this, a sense that this was where I belonged. I made my
way back up to the Cathedral and found it open. There was
only the verger there. The whole building was quiet, still. I
walked around, slowly, my eyes drinking in the coloured
stone, the curves, the heights, the different spaces. My heart
quickened as I came near Cuthbert's tomb and had a deep
sense of joining myself with pilgrims throughout the ages.
The sense of stillness and connectedness remained with me
for much of the day.

The third memory was in the summer of 1994. Nina had
been unexpectedly invited to spend three weeks with the family of a school friend in France, a time which coincided with
Sirpa's mother's seventieth birthday. The two of us flew to
Finland for three weeks, a country which in many ways had
been closed to us because of particular childhood experiences
suffered by Sirpa. As well as visiting relatives, we decided to
take some space for ourselves and were able to spend a few
days in a lodge in the woods overlooking a lake. The water
was so pure that it was piped straight into the house. We
swam with a local family of beavers, wandered through the
woods collecting berries, and luxuriated in the wood-heated
sauna, running out along the pier and diving straight into the
cool, refreshing lake water whenever it became too hot.

One day we went for a drive heading towards Savonlinna,
a big town and tourist centre. We never made it because of
the places we discovered along the way, one of which was the
site of ancient rock paintings. It was a mile from the nearest

road. We wended our way through woodland and lakeland, up and down little hills, with the trees thinning every so often to reveal views of other distant hills and then enveloping us again in their primeval warmth. At places the path was a jumbled web of interlacing root systems, each spot crying out to be contemplated because of the quality of the texture and shapes. Eventually we came down a steep hillside to the edge of the huge lake, which stretches for miles. There they were, huge, immense rocks towering up above us with scraggy little trees clinging perilously to their sides, and above us the paintings – animals, symbols and figures going back thousands of years.

Spontaneously Sirpa stripped off and dived into the lake. I followed more slowly and cautiously. From there the paintings in the context of the immensity of the rock became clearer, and we gently floated, lost in a sense of awe and wonder until driven out by a gradual coldness seeping through. For both of us there was deep sense of our having been in a sacred place, a feeling that the whole area was holy ground. We were not surprised therefore to encounter a particularly rare breed of snake on our way back. We experienced the visit to Finland as being one where deeply wounded memories were healed. Somehow that particular place seemed to have a central part in the healing process in a way that we both felt but couldn't analyse.

Shaping the journey

It was this deep sense of natural places feeding me at key points in my journey through life that came to mind when I was offered the chance to spend four months on 'sabbatical'. With the strong resonance that my experience of Celtic Christianity had evoked in me, the picture which came to my mind was of a journey through the countryside of the British

Isles, exploring this deep sense of God mediated through particular places in nature. One of the purposes of a sabbatical is
renewal, and it had been places like that that I had experienced as being deeply renewing. But behind the desire to visit
special places were deeper questions. Although I was drawn
to Celtic Christianity, nourished by it and leading workshops
to introduce people to it, at the same time I was questioning
it. I needed to explore the questions, 'What is this about? Is
this a Christian way of understanding the world which has
the power to heal the splits we make and give us a holistic
vision that will carry us into the next millennium? Is that why
it speaks so powerfully now to many? Or is this some sort of
romantic sentimental avoidance of the issues which face our
world and a means of escape from the harsh reality of our
lives? Are we simply mirroring the romantic Celtic revival of
the last century, or are we rediscovering something essential
about our roots and the roots of Christian faith in these
islands which is a vital step to our moving forward into a
different world, which will be a world of the imagination and
creativity alongside the rational which has so dominated our
thinking and theology over the past centuries? What about
people who live in the inner cities who have little access to the
countryside? Is Celtic Christianity something only for affluent
people with time to spend in rural recreation?'

  Linked with questions about Celtic Christianity were
questions about what has come to be called the 'new age
movement', a collection of very different groupings and
movements which point toward new ways of living and
being. I had been fascinated by the growth and the way that
the shelves in bookshops seemed to be expanding with 'new
age' books, while those on Christianity seemed to be shrinking. Most Christian writing on the 'new age' seemed to be
highly critical and to see it as a dangerous phenomenon to be
avoided at all costs. At the same time I was meeting a number

of people involved in different aspects of 'new age', and my wife was working in complementary medicine, doing remedial massage. The people I met struck me as being serious seekers, frequently people who had left the Church because it seemed to have nothing to say to their search for a depth of spirituality, who were finding the 'new age' offering more holistic ways of expressing their longing for a sense of God or the 'other' which affirmed the body and emotions as well as the mind and the spirit. They struck me as being far removed from the stereotypes of 'new age people' that were presented by Christian writers. This stereotyping came home to me when we were preparing a course on healing and asked the Diocesan healing panel for guidelines. In the paper they wrote traditional medicine was completely vindicated because of its rationalistic basis, whereas all forms of alternative medicines were to be viewed with deep suspicion because, for example, evil could enter people's bodies through acupuncture needles. This seemed to be a caution bordering on paranoia, which made me curious to explore the truth for myself.

I had always been wary of what seemed to be 'alternative' religions and spiritualities. My evangelical formation had taught me to be deeply suspicious of anything that wasn't 'sound' and didn't have the right language and doctrine. But a shift had taken place in me through an accident. In 1993, just before Christmas, I had fallen, breaking my right arm. I was unable to work, write, do practical jobs. So I had six weeks in which I read and prayed. I discovered how powerful silent meditation can be. I vividly remember walking into our local library and seeing bookshelves full of books about other religions and new age movements and feeling deep down inside, 'I don't need to be afraid of these'. I read voraciously and found myself touched by so much wisdom in what I read that seemed deeply in accord with much Christian understanding. At the same time there were all sorts of questions posed for me in what I was reading but it felt as though I had stepped out on to a new part of my journey of exploration into God, one that was full of a greater richness and variety than I had dreamt of.

What was more, I had experienced 'new age' activities like sacred (circle) dance as being deeply moving and enriching of my Christian spirituality. My first experience had been on a Christian conference where two Quakers led us in simple circle dances, and I found myself engaged in an activity which led me into a deep worship in which I felt the wonder of the depth of love of God in a new way. And yet I was reading Christian books which condemned circle dancing as being evil and in the same category as witchcraft. I had also started reading books about 'earth mysteries', the idea that the earth is a living being, full of energy, so that at particular places we can tap into that energy in renewing ways. This seemed to chime with my experience and I found a 'Yes' welling up to much of what I was reading. I was also aware that some of the new age groupings draw on Celtic mythology and imagery. So I had the idea of a journey which would explore the Celtic Christian tradition in the context of its current revival, and aspects of 'the new age movement', seeking to identify the links and differences between them. I thought of spending time in particular places, of taking the opportunity of going back to Ireland, of visiting Iona, Glastonbury, Stonehenge and Avebury. I thought of spending time at the new age centre of Findhorn, of spending time doing sacred circle dance.

However, the more I thought about it, the bigger it seemed to become, especially as I had the opportunity to focus it in the form of a dissertation for a Master's Degree in Applied Theology. It was then that the theme of 'sacred space' came to me. That was what it seemed I had experienced in my various encounters with God in nature, a sense that there was something about that particular place, that particular spot, which had something of 'sacredness' about it. That seemed to be a focus for the revival of interest in places like Iona and Lindis-farne in the Celtic tradition, people feeling that there was a quality about those places which made pilgrimage to them worthwhile and important to do. That also seemed to be a focus for the revival of 'new age' interest in places like Stonehenge and Glastonbury.

And then it struck me that that was one way of conceiving the role of the Church in society – as a holder of sacred space for people. Wasn't that what church architecture was partly about – the creation of a specific 'sacred' space through a particular type of building, which when it was effective had the impact of a Durham cathedral? I made a connection with some of the experiences I had had, for example in circle dancing, which to me had a deep sense of sacredness about them. Wasn't ritual in whatever context about the creation of 'sacred space'? And what about those moments in the experience of a group when a silence seems to fall and everyone has a deep sense of this being a special moment, a sacred moment, that the group wants to hang on to and no one wants to be the one to break? Was that not also an experience of 'sacred space'?

And so my mind began to tease around the question of what makes for sacred space. What is it about some places which seem to give them that quality? Why do some places attract that sort of attention and not others? How do we explain the way that some sites seem to be recognised as being special both in pre-Christian and Christian traditions? And are there important clues here about the role of the Church in society today and its mission? How do we read the growth of 'new age' activity on the one hand, and the rise of charismatic, fundamentalist house church Christianity on the other, in contrast to the decline of numbers in the established churches? Could it be an indication that the Church is no longer seen as fulfilling its historic role as being a holder of sacred space for people, so that they are looking elsewhere?

I also wanted to explore the biblical background. I was aware of two themes running through Scripture. One is that God is present everywhere, that there is no need for special places, that God is found in the people who are faithfully seeking to follow the Christian way. The other is that special places are important as a particular focus of God's presence. So it is no coincidence that the transfiguration of Jesus takes place on a holy mountain which already has associations with Moses and Elijah, and the gospel writers are at pains to tell us not only what happened but where it happened. Many people who have been on pilgrimage to Israel come back glowing from their experience of the actual places where Jesus lived and died. There has been a tradition of pilgrimage to holy sites more or less throughout Christian history. Even sections of the Church which might think of pilgrimage as being something very 'catholic' and unbiblical seem to be rediscovering a sense of the importance of place, with the marches for Jesus which are about 'claiming places for God'. And Christians believe in a God who as well as being transcendent, apart from the world, is also immanent, having entered it fully in the person of Jesus Christ who lived in a specific place at a specific time, and who has a continuing intimate involvement in the world. So I wondered what part sacred places have in the Christian tradition and what their role is for us today.

The more I thought about it the more excited I became about exploring this area and using 'sacred space' as the focus. I found that when I talked about it to other people most responded with an enthusiasm and fascination and often, unprompted, would begin to tell me of their experiences of particular places, natural and religious, and of the way they had spoken to them. And so I resolved to use the sabbatical period as a journey of exploring sacred space practically and reflectively. It would be a pilgrimage to sacred places in which I would reflect on what was happening to me as I visited, and how that related to the experiences of thousands of others who make similar journeys.

Above all I wanted to deepen the experience of God that I was discovering through quiet meditation that seemed to contrast so strongly with what one writer has described as the 'all speaking, all singing, all activity' church.[1] I believed that visiting sacred places might deepen that for me and might be an experience of moving into a different space spiritually. At the same time I wanted to go with as few preconceptions as possible but open to whatever the journey might bring, and wherever God might choose to appear.

Little did I realise where the journey would lead. Little did I appreciate that a journey into sacred space out there would also be a journey into the inner space within and how dangerous that journey can feel for a man of forty-five, living a life that is outwardly effective and successful but inwardly is a turmoil. Little did I realise that an exploration into 'sacred space' might prove to be an exploration into darkness as much as into light. Had I realised what it was to involve I might never have embarked on the journey. But at the same time a bit of me knows that I could not have avoided it. I would have had to have faced it at some point. I had the feeling that this was something I had to do.

Note

1. Peter Stanford in *Sunday Times*, 21st Jan 1996

2

Getting Things Together

O the mind, mind has mountains; cliffs of fall
Frightful, sheer, no-man-fathomed
Gerard Manley Hopkins[1]

When my spirit is faint within me, you are there to
watch over my steps.
Psalm 142:3

Obstacles in the way

It proved far more difficult to get things together than I
expected. I found myself planning in the depths of the winter
months, which is generally a low time for me. On Sunday
29th January I wrote in my journal.

Last week was Sirpa's birthday and the fourth anniversary of
my mother's death. Not surprising if I feel low energy and
low motivation but I still struggle with it and feel there is so
much to do, so much I want to do. My work consultant felt I
am disengaging from my work role – he picked up the low
energy, low interest and when he questioned me I said I didn't
know what at the moment could energise me. A few months
ago it was spirituality, meditation, Celtic spirituality, creating
sacred space for people. Now, I don't know at all and it feels
as though nothing does. He felt that I was disengaging in

*order to prepare for the sabbatical which he sees at some level
as entering into and engaging with darkness. So many things
seem to be coming to a head somehow, and there seems
nowhere to go, no clear future. I still have a very deep sense of
not wanting to engage with people, not being in touch with
my feelings when I am with people, not daring to allow
myself to feel anything much, but just carrying on through
life, going through the motions of working, running with the
occasional bursts of energy I feel, but overall sensing a deep
pointlessness in everything. I can't get excited about my sabbatical even. I am clear that I should not plan it too much . . .
even writing doesn't excite me. God, how depressing I sound!*

I decided that I would make a trial visit to a sacred site experi-
menting with using a Dictaphone to record what I was
experiencing at each place visited. I chose to go to a stone
circle called Moel Ty Uchaf in north Wales. At one level the
visit was a failure. I woke up that morning with a headache
which persisted for most of the day. I followed the instructions
in the book where I had read about the site, but managed in
the mist to walk right past the circle, carrying on for miles up
a bleak, windswept mountainside. I slipped and fell in the
mud; further on I went into a bog over one boot which filled
with water. When I eventually found the circle on my way
back I was cold, tired, fed up and disappointed to find a circle
of tiny stones instead of the Stonehenge size of structure that
I had expected. When I tried to listen to the Dictaphone I
could hardly hear my voice for the noise of the wind.

And yet the experience was beginning to teach me about
sacred space. You can't rush into it – if you do, you miss it.
In order to see it I had to step aside from the different worlds
I was ascending through. As long as my attention was on putting one foot in front of the other I passed by it. There had to
be a stopping, a letting go, a conscious decision to step aside,
to 'be still'. And I missed it because I wasn't paying attention

to the map I had. Sacred spaces have their own geography, their own way of marking themselves out. I had to learn to read those, to take sacred space on its own terms, rather than deciding where I expected it to be, or how I expected it to be.

I found that the nearer I got to the period of the sabbatical, the harder it became to put anything in place. At one point it seemed I had endless possibilities. As I got nearer they all disappeared so that it was beginning to look alarmingly like four months with a great void in it. I found myself coping with feelings of guilt. It was all very well for me to be planning this pilgrimage but what right had I to have this time to myself, especially if it ended up being paid for out of contributions made by hard-pressed church members? What right had I to go off and leave the family for so long? What right had I to go and leave my colleagues coping with all the work that would continue to come in? I found it difficult to see what shape could be given to the thesis I hoped to write. What had seemed an important and worthwhile journey of exploration was beginning to look like a hare-brained idea. I began to feel stressed about planning the journey, so that what was supposed to be a time of relaxation and refreshment was becoming another source of pressure.

Companions for the journey

However, it was as I was sinking deeper into despair that I met my first major encouragement and began to find companions for the journey. Alan Shepherd, who runs a Creation Spirituality book service, put me in touch with a Sister Mary June, writing 'In the context of sacred space you will enjoy her discovery of Celtic spirituality during her months on a Hebridean island.' So I summoned up enough energy to ring her and arranged to visit.

I cycled out to her convent, which turned out to be a rather ugly mishmash of a building. I was met by a short, slightly round sister, who assured me that Sister was expecting me, rang a set number of buzzes on a buzzer (clearly a 'Come in Sister June' signal) and showed me into a sitting room. I sat down and waited, finding myself surprisingly calm. When Mary June appeared I felt an instant connection with her at an emotional level as though we could have kissed in greeting though never having met before. She struck me as being tall, handsome and a very centred person. The room we were in was a dizzying mass of colours and styles, with purple chairs, a dark carpet, a busy blue rug, bright yellow lampshades with tassels hanging down, an extraordinary variety of pictures on the walls ranging from modern art to ancient etchings, with wavy wall paper. And yet Mary June held my focus all the time with her contained energy, quiet intensity, and vigorous hand movements which were always purposeful and never wasted.

She clearly wasn't a person to engage in chitchat so I launched straight in with what I was hoping to explore. She asked me what sort of places I found sacred, and I had a feeling of being tested to see whether I was on the right wavelength. I was reassured by her nods as I talked of my experiences at Cissington Ring, of the waterfall and Lindisfarne. In response she shared her experiences of the island of Erraid where she lived with an ecological 'new age' community for two years, her feeling of the power of places associated with St Cuthbert; she spoke of links with ancient mystery religions and how she had lost her fear of them when she had hesitantly entered into a meditation leading her to a goddess figure, had found that her guide was Jesus, and had a sense of ancient mystery religions longing to be embraced by Christianity. As she spoke, I sensed a fellow traveller, someone who was walking on the borders and seeking to make sense of her experiences in the light of the Christian tradition, experiencing a deep connection of masculine and feminine energies and finding herself in an uncomfortable place not quite fitting into either world.

For the first time, I found myself describing to another person my experience of feeling drawn into worship at the sight of the full moon at a greater depth than I experience in church worship, and I found my eyes filling with tears as I spoke, tears both of relief and of longing and desire to find ways of expressing that part of myself. She shared an experience of doing a 'moon meditation' about which she had been very hesitant but which had been followed by seeing the moon as she had never seen it before, a great disc of white, and feeling God saying 'yes' to her through the moon.

Through all this I had the impression of a razor-sharp mind which would not tolerate any woolly thinking, and which sought to put any experience into a wider frame, for her a Christian one. She knew of an island where I could spend several days in solitude. When I left I had the feeling that I had found a 'soul friend', someone who really understood the journey I was making, who was in tune with the things that mattered to me, someone who had taken something of a similar journey before me. I later rang her and asked her if she would be prepared to 'walk with me' on the journey in a spiritual way, and be someone I could talk with to make sense of what was happening to me as I travelled, someone who could help me through the dangers as I plunged into the darkness of the exploration. I was thrilled when she said 'yes'. She has been a good companion, and from this point on more and more things began to fall into place for the journey.

The conversation with her seemed to put me in touch with deep inner emotions, so that a few days later I found myself crying when I read a description of Mother Earth as the one who sustains all growing things, who is the body, our bones and cells and who is found in the world around us in the

cycles, seasons of nature, and in mind, body, spirit and emotions within each of us. It seemed to touch a deep place of
connectedness between myself and the earth. It was the beginning of touching a part of myself that feels very vulnerable, a
feeling reinforced by a frightening experience which happened
shortly afterwards when I cycled to the Otterspool woods. It
was a mild but windy day, and I felt a surge of energy as I saw
the daffodils pushing their way up. I found myself noticing
the wonderful formations made by the bark of a tree which
had bulbous growths and huge curving lines running up and
down it. A little further on, I noticed a perfect circle of
daffodils around some flattened grass, like a mysterious fairy
ring. But then I found myself the object of attention from a
tall man, with blond hair caught up in a pony tail. I felt
vaguely disturbed, a mixture of fear and excitement. I moved
off, but became afraid when I noticed him following me.
Perhaps I was imagining it. I hurried on; he hurried after me.
When I stopped and looked back I could feel that he was
wanting to connect, and I felt that his desire was sexual. I was
afraid to confront him, afraid to cross his path. The path I
was on led out into a playing field. I cycled across it, grateful
for the speed the bike gave me. When I glanced back, he was
standing at the edge of the wood watching. I came to the gate
which led on to the road, but it was locked. The fence was tall
with spikes. I did not dare turn back – perhaps he was
dangerous? – so with my heart pounding I hauled the bicycle
over the fence, and scrambled up myself, my fear overcoming
any natural caution, as I dropped thankfully on to the safety
of the other side. I began to wonder why that had happened.
Was it a warning of the dangers I was opening myself up to?
I had never felt so vulnerable. I was frightened both by the
event and by the sexual excitement that I felt mixed in with
the fear. Was exploring sacred space going to expose me to
aspects of my personality that I didn't want to face?

Alan Shepherd had given me the name of another contact, James Stewart, one-time senior lecturer and now visiting lecturer in Creation Spirituality at Newcastle University. I travelled to Newcastle to meet him and discovered a shy man in his mid sixties with white hair, a neatly trimmed white beard, and glasses, dressed informally in corduroys and a sweater. He is someone who from a strong Christian background now believes the Church to be largely a fearful institution, frightened and stuck. Many churches resist any sense of God in nature because if the world outside is considered to be sacred then clergy lose their power to control sacred space. The result is that churches become clubs existing for their own members rather than places who accept people as they are. I could recognise signs of what he was describing in some of the churches I have worked with and could see ways in which the fear of God in nature lay within myself as much as in the institution.

My third visit turned out to be the most electrifying of all. I had been put in touch with a Brother Ramon, a Franciscan monk who was pursuing a call to be a hermit within the context of a religious order. As I had had a deep sense the previous year that had I not chosen to marry and have children I would like to explore such a vocation, I was intrigued to meet him, especially as my contact had suggested he would be very helpful both on the subject of sacred space and also in pointing me towards possible publishers. I then came up against the obstacle of how one gets to meet a hermit. For a start he wasn't on the phone. I saw a space in my diary (a rare occurrence!) and wrote hoping he might be able to see me, but he wrote back explaining that he had 'gone over his "ration" of people during the last two months'. He suggested that I came a day early and spent the night in the monastery, and proposed some dates later in the year. I was able to make one of them, so wrote to confirm, and had a letter back which I found somewhat directive but which also made me smile:

'Depending on your arrival we could meet on Sunday after-noon/evening, but I think it might be a good idea for you to settle in and get the feel of the monastery, and look around the library, spending some time in the chapel, in preparation for our meeting on Monday. If you came down to me at about 10.00 ... I suggest that after some words of greeting we might spend perhaps 15 minutes in my chapel hut quietly before the Lord, then have some coffee and launch into our session together.' He sent me a list of directions ending with 'At monastery, go up side path to guesthouse door, ring and guestbrother will bring you down to Ramon. (Loo at guest-house entrance).'

I travelled down on the Sunday via Antony's school, which happens to be nearby and where he was taking part in a cross country inter-school run. Antony is our son. He has a complex of learning difficulties, emotional and behavioural problems. We had always struggled in living with him at home, and three years previously he had moved to a residential Rudolph Steiner school where he has made tremendous progress. The move has transformed our relationship with him, so that we now look forward to his visits home, something which at one time would have been inconceivable. I had been very impressed that they had got him running, and was a little disillusioned to find myself standing in a slushy, snow-covered field watching him walk most of the way while staff shouted, 'Come on Antony, run,' to no avail.

I made my way through desolate Worcestershire coun-tryside up a little track to the monastery, which looked bleak and forbidding. There were hardly any lights on. Over the main door were the words, 'There stood by the cross of Jesus his mother', which somehow seemed out of place. A brother materialised in answer to my bell, but had to disappear to preach, so I was left to wait for another to appear. I was led around long, narrow, dark corridors which were freezing cold, shown an uninviting, cold, chapel, and an area which he described as 'the black hole, into which you may not go because it's private'. I was also told to be silent in the corridors. My room was freezing, though there was a small fan heater I was able to put on and huddle by. It had a high ceiling out of all proportion to its width, which gave it an eerie feel. I began to wonder what sort of place I had come to. I obeyed Ramon's instructions and tried to read in the library but it was too cold. The chapel service was uninspiring and seemed endlessly wordy to me. It was with some relief that I discovered tea being shared in a cheerful little sitting room with a log fire and huge slabs of homemade cake. I went to bed with my sweater and socks on, and only began to feel better when I woke to a sunny morning.

At the appointed time guestbrother appeared to take me down to Ramon. I had very clear ideas of the person I was going to meet. He had chosen to live in solitude so he would be a quiet, reserved, person, full of deep wisdom. I expected long silences, out of which would come pearls. It would be a reflective time during which my deepest motives would be placed under the searchlight, and I would emerge knowing who I am and what I am about. I was totally unprepared for what I encountered. As soon as we arrived outside the hut Ramon appeared, seeming to bark instructions to guestbrother. Then he whisked me inside, talking incessantly, making coffee, and spitting in his enthusiasm to get words out. I suddenly found myself faced by a fiery Welshman with the 'gift of the gab' and an ability to weave pictures with stories, an ex-evangelical Baptist who had lost none of his evangelistic zeal. Initially, I was taken aback but as the morning developed I discovered that I was with an open, gentle, questioning, questing soul who was able to listen sensitively and quick to pick up the essence of what I was saying. He

shared our disappointment in the falling through of a possibility for Sirpa to use a former church as a sacred space for
healing. He was aware of his fortune in being so free, and
deeply concerned that Sirpa and I found an appropriate way
forward to exercise our gifts. It seemed that he was almost
disappointed not to have been able to discern our future path
by the end of our conversation.

The hut was appropriately simple with books, cooker, two
chairs, a bed with a brightly coloured bedspread, and a window looking out over the countryside. Ramon shared his
deep sense as a young boy that God was in the whole of
nature and was 'bigger' than himself. When he discovered
Jesus it transformed the sense of God in nature into love, so
for him there was no quarrel between the two. He also talked
of the Church's fear of 'nature', which he believes is because
nature is powerful and mysterious and touches our sexuality
and creativity, and religious people and institutions find that
hard to handle. So the Christian tradition teaches us grace
over against nature, but Jesus did not express a fear of nature.
Ramon sees the prophets as mystics, aware of God in nature
all around them, just as Moses experienced God in the burning bush. He spoke of human beings as priests of creation,
and the role of the Church as being to lead people deeper into
their humanity as creatures of God, and spoke with passion
of a place that is special for him, a church in Wales which has
been a place of pilgrimage for centuries.

He introduced me to the world of Duncton Wood, a series
of books by William Horwood about the world of moles, in
which he weaves spiritual wisdom and Christian symbolism
into a totally engrossing saga of hope and light overcoming
the most horrendous forces of darkness and evil.[2] The focus
of the faith of the true moles is a series of holy stones and particularly the 'silence of the stone', a state of being of pure faith
and trust. The books accompanied me on my journey and I

found myself struck time and time again by the parallels with my own experience. Ramon himself is an author of devotional books, and I took one of his called *Forty Days and Forty Nights*, with me on the travels.[3] He offers a theme, Bible passage and reflection for each day, and almost always I found something of depth and relevance in what he wrote. I left feeling that I had met another companion and fellow traveller, one who understood the exploration I was undertaking, a sense borne out in my subsequent correspondence with him.

Piece by piece aspects of the journey were falling into place. It would start with a visit to Glastonbury and an exploration of sacred places around the area, including Stonehenge and Avebury. From there I would travel to Scotland to spend eight days in solitude on an uninhabited island, one of the Garvellachs, and follow that with a week celebrating midsummer with circle dancing at the 'new age' community at Findhorn. I would travel up to the edge of Scotland and spend a few days visiting sites on Orkney before following in the footsteps of St Ninian on the Whithorn peninsula in south west Scotland and St Cuthbert in the east border country and Northumbria. Then the journey would take me down to south west Wales and the area around St David's, and finish by joining the tens of thousands of pilgrims who climb the mountain of Croagh Patrick in south west Ireland on the last Sunday of July.

However, there was another hurdle to overcome, which was the leaving of work. I hadn't realised how difficult it would be to unbind the cords which tie me to it. I anticipated my last day as being a joyful one, a sense of being 'de-mob' happy. Instead, I woke up with a headache, feeling rotten. I went into work to find that one of my colleagues had organised a mysterious 'leaving' party. I was kept waiting and then led into one of the conference rooms. As I walked in there were bangs, and balloons and a room full of people. I was handed an envelope with quotes and anonymous messages in it. I think the idea was that I was meant to weave a story of my life around them. I felt embarrassed, awkward, uncomfortable and wanting to hide. I agreed to answer questions, but everyone else seemed equally embarrassed, until Anne, my secretary, set the ball rolling. Eventually I was allowed to open a big box, which turned out to have an iced cake with a bicycle and a tent on it and the phrase 'On your bike, Chris'. I laughed with delight when I saw it, and during the afternoon my headache cleared. It felt as though I was being given permission to go away. At the same time I was beginning to worry at the number of people who were saying, 'We look forward to seeing you when you come back ... *if* you come back, that is', almost as though they knew something I didn't. It seemed to underline that I was doing no small thing in deciding to explore sacred space; that the interior journey might lead me anywhere and even make it impossible for me to come back. Only time would tell.

But before embarking on the journey proper I had three practice runs into 'sacred space'. I had heard of Holy Island, a little island off-shore which has been bought by Tibetan Buddhists and is being reclaimed by them as a place of prayer and retreat. I wanted to visit it so I rashly suggested taking the children camping there over Easter. I had always thought there was just one 'Holy Island', Lindisfarne, off the Northumberland coast. I was discovering that the British Isles are ringed with a number of them. Once I realised what I was taking on, with a thirteen-year-old who is becoming snooty about camping, and a fifteen-year-old lad with learning difficulties, wetting problems and an ability to drive everyone up the wall within minutes, I invited a friend to come with us, Giles David, who had recently finished his contract with the Iona community and was 'resting' between posts.

We quickly discovered that we had made a mistake in accepting another friend's generous offer of an additional tent. I should have listened more carefully when he kept on insisting, 'There's nothing wrong with the fly sheet.' There wasn't, but the tent leaked abominably! There was also a freezing cold wind blowing most of the time we were there. There was one boat a day across to Holy Island and we decided to go the next day. We took the scenic route, thinking we had plenty of time, when we suddenly realised we didn't. Hurrying on windy Scottish roads is not easy, particularly when you get behind slow vehicles. Giles' rising anxiety did not help. 'You're going to have to get past this one,' he shouted, as we crawled behind a particularly slow lorry. 'I know that, you idiot,' I felt like shouting back, but pursed my lips, and concentrated on peering round every bend until I could see a chance. 'Right, we'll have to be ready to jump out as soon as we arrive,' Giles says, and there is a mad scramble as people try to find boots and coats and hats. We screech into the car park; Giles runs to get tickets; I push boots on to Antony's unyielding feet and we set off at a run. It hardly feels the right way to approach sacred space, which all the books had told me should be approached slowly, reverently, purposefully, not at a run worrying about all the things we might have left behind.

Once on the island something about it seems to take us over. It has a very evocative shape, with a rounded hill looking as though it is emerging out of the sea. We walk slowly along the sea, each in our own time and space, absorbing the nature, pausing to pick up a stone or piece of wood. We know there is a cave associated with St Molaise. We wonder if we will even find it or recognise it. Suddenly Giles gives a shout, and appears above us. Rough, stone steps lead up to where the ground levels off and forms the ledge of the cave, which runs for several metres either side. The floor is flat and paved. There is a ledge at the back. On it someone has placed a large stone with two simple jars and a small stone, forming a focus. We sit in quiet, none of us venturing to enter, aware of being at a holy place, feeling its calming effect on us, its invitation to silence, to be. Only after some time has elapsed do we venture to go into the cave, Giles first, adding a piece of coloured wool he carries with him to the altar. We feel a strong presence. It is a place to linger in.

The second practice run arose from discovering that the first day of my sabbatical, 1st May, coincided with the Celtic festival of Beltane, a significant date in the Celtic calendar. I had been reading the imaginary account in a book called the *The Sun and the Serpent* of people all along what is believed to be an energy line running from the tip of Cornwall to East Anglia, known as the Michael line, greeting the sunrise on this day every year with bonfires spreading across the line as the sun touched different places.[4] My imagination had been fired and I realised that I had never consciously watched the sun rise though I had seen it set many times, so I decided to mark the first day by getting up in the early hours to experience sunrise. I spoke into the Dictaphone as I watched.

All around the grass is liquid dew with a gentle white mist rising off it. Something very special about this time of day, something innocent, fresh, full of promise, hopefulness, particularly this moment at the beginning of Summer with its promise of new life, a renewing of the earth, a time of fertility with the sun caressing the earth. Sounds seem unusually clear. I am full of expectancy – when will it come? Where will its rays first strike? I am aware of the importance of places so carefully chosen, where the stones have been placed to mark the sanctuary on which the rays will fall as the sun appears. I feel tearful at the wonder of the new day. I can just begin to make out a reddening glow which seems to say, 'Be patient, I'm coming, wait.' Now it's coming, it's coming! I can see the golden ball filling the horizon, so bright I can hardly gaze at it. I feel a mixture of tearfulness, ecstasy and a sense that the earth, the grass, the trees, the birds are all greeting the sun, like a dance between earth and sun. I can't look any more. I close my eyes and the orb remains imprinted on them, becoming part of me. Now the sun disappears behind a cloud but it doesn't matter, it's there, nothing will be the same again. The sun has risen. The Son has risen with healing in his wings.

The third foray took place in Turkey. To bridge the gap between work and sabbatical journey I had decided to go on holiday with Sirpa which was how we came to find ourselves on a local bus making the fifteen-hour journey from Mamaris on the south coast to Cappadocia. The person due to take us from the hotel to the bus is late, and his car screeches up with minutes to spare. We pile in, and he hurtles off at breakneck speed, explaining the bus will wait for us; but can we believe it? Minutes later we skid into the bus station, halting by a huge coach. People rush up, 'Are these the English?' and our bags are put on, we haul ourselves up, and barely have time to find our seats before the bus is off at high speed. It is packed, mainly with local people. It rapidly fills with thick, sweet cigarette smoke, making the atmosphere heavy. Whenever we are about to nod off we pull into a bus station for a break to stretch legs and buy refreshments. Whenever the atmosphere feels as though it is getting unbearable the conductor comes round with a bottle of perfumed water and we all hold our hands out expectantly like communicants at a eucharist. He pours great dollops into our hands which we rub all over our face and arms. For a few delicious moments the bus smells clean and sweet until the cloying smell of tobacco begins to clamp down again.

We arrive at the bus station at our destination, Neveshir, at four o'clock in the morning. Everyone else is met. No one for us. The bus station is deserted. We are high in the mountains. It is freezing cold, we are tired and hungry, and no one comes.

Sirpa is fighting cockroaches off our luggage, while I walk around desperately trying to stay warm. Eventually, we manage to get in touch with the local office – the person due to collect us has overslept.

From that moment on we find ourselves plunged into a fairy-tale world of experience after experience. The whole area is covered in a soft lava which forms contorted shapes, towering up into the sky forming a weird, moonlike landscape. Local people had discovered that the lava could be dug into, so had created villages, towns and churches out of the rock. We sit in underground living rooms, monastic cells, crawl down passageways of cities seven storeys underground where thousands of Christians hid for up to a month at a time while continuing their baptising and teaching; walk along rushing rivers in deep wooded gorges; make friends with a Turkish couple on holiday from Istanbul; and visit church after church where frescoes painted in natural dyes still have their original colour and wonderful primitive style. Every day brings new delights and surprises. It is here that I discover the effect crowds of tourists can have on sacred places. As they rush in, look around, take photos, listen to guides and rush on, they seem to suck the energy and atmosphere out of the places. I find myself praying, crossing myself before each altar, offering something into the place which by its atmosphere of prayer over centuries is giving me so much. I feel a desire to honour the places I visit, to acknowledge their specialness, to spend time in them, to offer myself up to their mystery.

Finally, after these initial forays which felt almost like practice skirmishes, a way of getting into training as a walker might do day walks before setting out on an expedition, I was ready to set out on the journey proper. I knew where I was going and had some sense of why I was going. At the same time it felt important to be setting out without preconceiving what I might discover. It felt important to be open to the experience whatever it might hold for me. The hallway was full of camping equipment, clothes, books and food as I said my farewells to Sirpa and Nina and went to bed in our spare room so as to slip away in the early hours. I slept uneasily as I wondered what was to come.

Notes

1. *Poems and Prose of Gerard Manley Hopkins*, selected by WH Gardner, Penguin 1953, p27
2. *Duncton Wood, Duncton Quest* and *Duncton Found*, William Horwood, Arrow
3. *Forty Days and Forty Nights*, Brother Ramon, Marshall Pickering
4. *The Sun and the Serpent*, H Miller and P Broadhurst, Pendragon Press 1989

PART 2

The Journey

3

Connecting Earth and Heaven

From world to world there is a needle's eye.
Kathleen Raine[1]

A ladder which rested on the ground with its top reaching to heaven.
Genesis 28:12

Bredon Hill

I woke at five o'clock, to a perfect summer's morning with warm, hazy sunshine. The laburnum in the front garden was in its yellow glory as I carried innumerable bags and boxes out to the car. As I drove off I was aware of a mixture of inner excitement combined with a sort of choked up feeling. I had decided to base myself at Glastonbury, a place I had never visited but which had loomed in something of a mystic cloud through much of my life. The more I had read about earth energies and earth mysteries, the more special it appeared to be and it felt like a magnet drawing me. The roads were quiet in the early morning and I enjoyed the experience of cruising around Birmingham in contrast to the more usual snarl ups as one crawls past the RAC traffic centre.

I had decided to explore Bredon Hill on the way. The previous year while on a conference in a nearby house I had noticed that the hill was marked on my road atlas as having an iron age hill fort, abbey and spring nearby, all hallmarks of sacred places. I had mentally marked it down as a place to visit, and then by one of those curious happenings that you know inside is more than coincidence I had received through the post an earth mysteries magazine. The main article had been a description of Bredon Hill, which it described as also having the remains of a chapel dedicated to St Catherine next to a holy well, a sacred stone called the Elephant stone at the top, and two other sacred stones known as the King and Queen stones which were apparently used well into the last century as the venue of a 'court leet' in which the clerk of the court would ask permission of the stones to open the court. I could feel its call as a place which was recognised in pre-Christian and Christian times as being special.

The nearest town is Pershore so I made for it to see what information I could glean from the library. I found myself in a

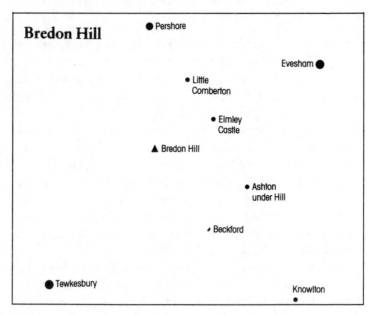

beautiful ancient town dominated by its Abbey. I walked across the grassy lawns which surround the ancient place of worship, dotted with trees near which a few locals were enjoying the sunshine on carefully positioned benches. I stepped out of the sunshine into a narrow porch with its doors and muted light which began to slow me down. But even that did not prepare me for entering a most wonderful space of simple beauty, symmetry and light. Almost instantly, I found myself being slowed down further to a deep sense of inner quiet. It was the first of many experiences of finding myself surprised by unexpectedly coming across a sacred site.

It was here that I first encountered the 'Green Man', a cheerful face carved in stone, peering down from the roof, with leaves and rich foliage coming out of his mouth. The Abbey notes stated, 'The Green Man was an Earth God who became entwined with the Christian religion. He is recognised as a life force. Jack of the Green, dressed in leafy twigs, was always found at the May celebrations.' This was the first of several 'Green Men' that I was to find in my travels, carved on ceilings and arches and floors of churches. In my innocence, I believed that I had found my first piece of evidence of celebration of nature at the heart of early Christian faith, especially when I discovered some churches where the guides seemed deliberately to omit any reference to the 'Green Man', even when one was grinning down at me, as though wanting to cover it up. It was only later that I came across a book by Dr Ron Hutton of Bristol University which pointed out that the Green Man was almost certainly a warning against what happened if you indulged in lust, and the link with 'Jack of the Green' was totally spurious, the latter character having only appeared in the late eighteenth century as part of a romantic revival movement which invented 'pagan' customs![2] I was beginning to discover that I was entering a world where historians disagree forcibly and where speculation runs riot.

In the library I was alerted to the large number of churches of Saxon origins which lie around the base of the hill, so I set off to visit them. Each name seemed to tell a story. St Peter's Little Comberton, St Mary's Elmley Castle, St Barbara's Ashton, St John the Baptist's Beckford. In each it was as though time seemed to have stood still, with open churches nestling in villages of stone mansions and cottages. At Beckford I was startled by the carving in the porch. It was of a cross with a bird on one of its arms and what looked like a sun or moon over the other with what could be unicorns. As I gazed at it I was aware of being in the presence of something ancient and significant. The guidebook described two theories which had been offered. One was that the sun was an eye representing the Father, the cross the Son and the bird the Holy Spirit which seemed to me an artificial attempt to make the carving appear orthodox. The other was that they represented the sacred beasts of the Celts paying homage to the new religion represented by the Cross. This fitted the picture I later discovered of a remarkably easy transition from the pre-Christian Celtic religion to Christianity, as though the earlier religion recognised in the new one a fulfilment of its beliefs rather than an opposition to them. However, some scholars question the ease of this transition. Once more I was discovering that there are debates raised and unanswered questions about nearly everything to do with the Celtic and mediaeval church.

Bredon Hill rises prominently from the surrounding landscape. It looked as though it would be straightforward to find a road up. It wasn't. Some roads seemed to disappear before they reached the hill while others were plastered with 'No parking' signs put up by local people. Once on the hill it was difficult to find a route up. For not the first time I was discovering that sacred space can be difficult to get into. Eventually, I found my way up to the fort. As soon as I stepped through its grassy ramparts my breath started coming more quickly. I felt connected as though my body and feelings were suddenly in tune. In place of my weariness there was a joyful energy. The huge stone just under the ridge which surrounded the top seemed to give off energy. I came to a little hollow and crouched down and found myself feeling tearful, the sort of tearfulness which touches a vulnerable spot hidden somewhere near my stomach, where joy and sadness combine in strange harmony. However, all my attempts to find St Catherine's chapel and well proved fruitless on this and a subsequent occasion when I went back. Nor did I manage to find the King and Queen stones in spite of following the directions in the magazine to within feet of where they should have been, and wandering up and down grassy, briar-clad hillocks. I was discovering how elusive some sacred sites can be. On the way down I got wet in an unexpected shower and totally lost. I pride myself on having a good sense of direction and like to know exactly where I am going. As I rapidly lost confidence in my sense of where I was I was afraid that I might never find my way back to the car. I could see myself still wandering the hill at nightfall, with many more miles to travel before reaching Glastonbury. It was with some relief that I found my way down to some houses, but my relief quickly turned into dismay as two large dogs appeared barking ferociously, followed by a gruff looking man, cross at this unwelcome disturbance. I apologised for my intrusion and was pointed in the right direction, not daring to relax until I finally saw the car tucked into its tiny mud-hardened layby. Perhaps sacred space was going to be be harder to get out of than into!

Glastonbury

I felt very tired as I neared Glastonbury in persistent drizzly rain, but I did have a rush of blood as I saw the Tor, the rounded hill which rises up out of the Somerset plain, with its

striking tower on the top. The campsite I had picked out from
my guidebook turned out to be out of the sight of the Tor,
and the neatly organised tents huddled together felt claustro-
phobic. I turned back to another I had passed and was able to
pitch with the Tor rising up behind the tent, with a wide open
space in front and views across the plain to distant hills. I also
found myself camped alongside a fascinating mixture of
travellers, hippy types in old vans, ambulances and trucks
alongside established families on holiday. The woman who
took my money explained, 'We get all sorts here, but we all
get on like one big happy family.' I had to put the tent up
between showers, just managing before a heavy downpour. I
was aware of rehearsing for when I was to be in solitude for
eight days on the island. If I am struggling here where there is
no wind, how will I manage there? Here I could ask for help
from a neighbour, but there there will be no one to help. The
meals I have planned are also a test – will they work? Will I
be happy with this menu for eight days on my own?

   The next day was sunny and cold. The wind was too cold
to sit out, the sun too hot to be comfortable in the tent or car.
I was aware of making myself too much breakfast, how easy
it is to fall into gluttony when on my own, and resolved to
discipline my eating. Then I set off for the Tor, and Glastonbury. I felt peaceful and excited all at once, a sense of a real
beginning to this exploration into sacred space. I was there at
last, this place which had been in my consciousness for so
long. I walked up a tiny little narrow road, deserted of traffic,
with high wooded hedges bursting out with leaves and greenery, into a blaze of white and yellow meadowland. The
plaque at the bottom tells me that 'Tor' means 'hill', that it is
518 feet above sea level, that the tower is what remains from
a mediaeval church dedicated to St Michael, built to replace
a previous church which fell in an earthquake in the thir-
teenth century. Excavations have revealed traces of fifth- or

sixth-century buildings. It also says that the Tor has been for many a focus of magic, legend and superstition. In preparing, I have read about many of the legends – that Joseph of Arimathea came here when it was an island, planted his staff on Wearyall Hill which sprouted into a thorn tree, and founded the first Christian Church in these islands; that the Holy Grail, the communion cup used by Jesus, was buried here; that the Tor has on it an ancient maze, used for pagan rituals; that here St Collen did battle with Gwynn ap Nudd, the King of the Underworld; and more recently that two powerful energy lines, the Mary line and the Michael line, interweave around the Tor, forming the shape of a chalice or Grail joining the male and female energies in ancient symbolism.

As I stood by the plaque I could see the path winding its way around the hill above me, the skyline dominated by the tower stretching up, with its top seeming to disappear into the sky. I had a high sense of anticipation as I set out to climb up. I half expected every step I took to charge my body with supernatural energies. It didn't but when I reached the top I felt myself to be in a very special place. There was a deep

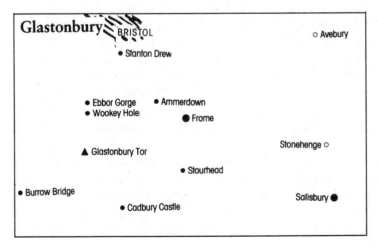

sense of inner grief combined with a sense of wholeness and renewal. All the time I was in the area the Tor acted as a magnet, drawing me back. I found myself drawn to climb it at least once each day. One evening I went up in the bitterly cold wind, and stood for hours watching as the sun set and the stars began to appear, the power of the place holding me in spite of the icy wind and the comments of other visitors. 'What's he on?' was one. I also observed its effect on others. Often people would arrive in a group, but then wander off on their own, as if drawn to commune with the place. One night, someone was sleeping out on the top; often people would sit playing drums. There was a wide variety of people of all ages dressed in conventional and new age styles. I talked with one older woman with a genteel accent who had always wanted to come, was thrilled to be there, who waved her hand over the landscape, saying 'Isn't it wonderful to think that Joseph of Arimathea walked around *here*?' I didn't have the heart to say that I thought it was very unlikely that he actually had.

I went on down to the Chalice Well which lies near the foot of the Tor. It is set in gardens bought by a Trust which maintains them as a sacred place of solitude, peace, healing, refreshment and renewal. On paying my pound entrance I found myself at what for me became the heart of Glastonbury's magic. The gardens are tiny and yet spacious. Everywhere there are hidden corners, arbours, benches under trees. The water pours from the well into troughs and pools running down through the gardens. It produces twenty five thousand gallons a day, and has never been known to dry up. The water is particularly high in iron content, giving it an unusual flavour and health-giving properties. People have come here for healing for hundreds, possibly thousands of years. On one day in 1751, ten thousand people are said to have visited. The remains of a yew tree dating from 300 AD have been found, along with mesolithic flints indicating a site of occupation for thousands of years. The yew tree is in line with more recently planted ones. If they replace earlier ones they may have formed an avenue of yews which is likely to have been used for ancient ritual. Whatever the facts of its history, it was for me a deeply special place. Even focused meditation felt too energetic, such was the sense of stillness it generated. It was a totally relaxing, absorbing atmosphere, so that the healing for me was not only in the waters but in the whole surroundings. Every so often as I dreamily moved around my eye was drawn to glimpses of the Tor dominating the landscape.

Eventually tearing myself away I walked on through the town, a mixture of new age and traditional shops, with 'travellers', tourists and locals appearing to mingle in easy toleration of one another. A Christian had spoken of finding Glastonbury 'spooky'. Only one place gave me that feel, a shop devoted to witchcraft and pagan ritual. My next visit was to the Abbey, and again I found myself on a site in which I could feel energies from the earth, a sense of stillness, and a deep awe at the majesty and scale of the buildings. The most electric sensation, however, was walking into the fourteenth-century Abbot's kitchen, which is virtually complete. I was in a space which moved me to tears with its simplicity and beauty. I suddenly became aware as I gazed in wonder that it had exactly the same shape as Mongolian gers or yurts – a circular wall rising straight up, then curving into a dome with ribs at intervals leading up to an 'eye of heaven', a round opening or window above the centre. Sirpa had been on a yurt making course, and had come back full of the sense of sacredness generated by their shape. I had visited one and been struck by its power to generate an immediate sense of sacredness, stillness and intimacy. And now I was in a place with the same shape and proportions built out of stone in the fourteenth century! Sacred geometry speaks of the way in which many created sacred places such as stone circles and temples appear to be representations of the cosmos, and here I was experiencing the power of a ribbed dome shape with what appeared as a representation of the sun at its heart. I was also struck by the quality of the light which came from the central opening, similar to that gained from a skylight but enhanced.

My initial exploration of Glastonbury ended with a visit to Wearyall Hill. I didn't feel any particular energy from the thorn tree, which was hung with bits of cloth, ribbon and a simple wooden cross, but did experience a sense of mystery about it. I stood looking over the town bathed in late afternoon sunshine, wondering about the power of the place. The town is quite ordinary in appearance. The Tor is striking, but not dramatic or awesome as many mountains are. And yet the whole place had a special atmosphere which kept drawing me back, reinforcing a sense that there are some places which have a 'sacredness' about them in and of themselves, something which it is difficult to explain or analyse but which is felt by thousands of people both today and through time.

Earth Mysteries

It didn't seem surprising, having spent time there, that Glastonbury is a place that has generated more myth and associations than anywhere else in England and has been a focus for speculations of every kind. People have seen all the twelve signs of the zodiac perfectly represented in the surrounding countryside; King Arthur is supposed to be buried in the Abbey; it is claimed that St Patrick was Abbot here. And now it has become the centre and focus for the 'earth mystery' movement. The popularised version of their belief is that underneath the earth run lines of energy which every so often cross. Where they intersect the energies are more accessible to humans, and such points were recognised by our ancient forebears who were more attuned to these energies than we are. It is at these cross over points that we find prehistoric megaliths, stone circles, standing stones, prehistoric burial mounds and more recently churches. The recently revived art of dowsing can help us to pick up these energies and trace the lines over the landscape. The lines are known as 'leys' or 'ley lines', the name stemming from the researches of Alfred Watkins, who in 1921 at the age of sixty-six had a flash of insight, suddenly realising that ancient sites existed in straight line alignments, with churches later being built exactly on them in perfect alignment. His ideas caught on, and an 'Old Straight Track Club' was formed to trace these alignments all over the country. The club closed in the 1940s and 'ley lines' dropped out of most people's consciousness, to be revived by the publication in 1963 of a book called *A View over Atlantis* by John Michell.[3]

John Michell is a well-read, mystical, energetic, enthusiastic, charismatic figure, who brings together a wealth of learning culled from different disciplines into a cohesive whole, in a way which has appealed to the popular imagination. It was he who first drew people's attention to the 'St Michael line', pointing out the remarkable number of megaliths and churches built on hills which appear to lie in a straight line stretching from St Michael's Mount in Cornwall, through Glastonbury, Avebury and Bury St Edmunds to Hopton on the East Anglian coast. He has also carried out a very detailed survey of an area of Cornwall, drawing attention to a large number of apparent alignments. *A View over Atlantis*, now updated as *A New View over Atlantis*, is a fascinating mixture of fact, folk lore, numerology and speculation. Precisely because he calls on so many sources and draws in parallels from all over the world it is very difficult to evaluate his work. It has come under wide criticism not only from

academics but from fellow enthusiasts like Paul Devereux.
What is indisputable is its appeal to the popular imagination.

I was struck by how many people I met in my travels for
whom 'ley lines' as energy lines were definite fact, things they
could sense in particular sites. These included not just people
at sites, whom one might expect to have such beliefs, but
other people from whom the mention of my area of exploration would elicit enthusiastic accounts of their experience of
ley lines and earth energies. What struck me in visiting Glastonbury, however, was how this whole 'mythology' has been
generated by a small band of people, often producing works
through tiny publishing houses run by enthusiasts, such as
Gothic Image in Glastonbury who also organise 'Avalon'
tours around the mysteries of Glastonbury, and Pendragon
Press based in Cornwall.

The mythology is very powerful. Sister June had told me
about the book *The Sun and the Serpent*.[4] It is the account by
two dowsers of their attempt to trace the 'St Michael' line. It
reads like a detective story in which they found not what they
were expecting to find, which could be explained away, but
something totally different and unexpected, which was
another energy line interweaving in and out of the Michael
line and combining with it at significant points, particularly
Glastonbury. They named it the Mary line and retraced their
steps to follow it from the beginning. Every time their dowsing seemed to be leading them off track they discovered
another 'St Mary' church, often hidden away, unknown but
with powerful energies and atmosphere and frequently
intriguing history. I found it fascinating and believable.
Others in the field, however, are now taking a very different
view and questioning the idea of earth energies. For example,
Paul Devereux, who has spent many years researching this
area, and edits the *Ley Hunter's Journal*, now believes that
'straight line alignments' are 'spirit paths' along which the

shamans would travel in their trances to gain knowledge of the 'otherworld' and bring back healing and wisdom.[5]

The irony is that the myth or reality of earth energy has so caught the public imagination that no amount of questioning seems likely to eradicate it. It is now forming the basis for many other understandings not connected with 'ley lines', such as that put forward in a book called *The Celestine Prophecy*, which has been a bestseller in the States and is set to become one in the UK.[6] It tells of the discovery of nine insights which form the new understanding to take us forward into a new human consciousness. The book argues that this will be the next stage of development in human kind and indeed is already happening. The key to this new consciousness is developing our ability to tap into the energy of the cosmos, which can transform our experience and the way in which we relate to one another, ending violence and war and reconnecting us with the earth and universe. Part of the powerful appeal of the book, particularly in the American context, is that it argues that this is a fundamentally Christian concept, so that the process of tapping into this energy is seen as a process of becoming more Christ-like.

At this stage in my journey I found myself experiencing the power of a particular place, Glastonbury, and having what felt like powerful experiences of the energy of the earth. At the same time I was finding that intellectually the whole concept of earth energy seemed to be built on shaky foundations, propagated by a small group of enthusiasts. In my reading and observations, however, I was experiencing something which seemed to be life-affirming and life-giving, and which therefore I could not dismiss as being contrary to Christian faith. I resolved to journey on, trusting God to lead me, holding on to a scepticism alongside an openness to what the journey might bring. It was time to do some reflection with other Christians.

Ammerdown

Another reason for starting my exploration in Glastonbury
was that the Christian Arts network were holding their
annual weekend conference at Ammerdown, a centre near
Bath, not far away, and they happened this year to have
chosen the theme of sacred space. Having pitched my tent so
close to the Tor I decided to leave it under the watchful eye of
my neighbour, a single woman with two young children,
while I made my way towards the relative luxury of a proper
bed and immediate access to showers. To my surprise I left
my tent full of regrets. Having begun to enjoy the walk
through the grass to the showers and wash basins, with its
sense of being part of nature, and the experience of cooking
outside, I was reluctant to re-enter 'civilisation'. But I was
intrigued to know what a group of Christian artists would
make of the theme of sacred space and how they might
approach it.

On my way I visited the mediaeval town of Wells and its
beautifully sited Cathedral, with its magnificent west front
which soars upwards replete with statues and stone carvings,
and went on to Wookey Hole, a huge series of caverns
occupied since prehistoric times, where St Bernard is said to
have done battle with the witch, turning her to stone. There
one can feel the presence of ancestral figures, particularly
standing near the cave used for worship and burials, a feeling
which stayed with me in spite of being lost in a maze of
mirrors battling my way through a mock Victorian fun fair in
my attempts to get back to the car. Driving on I noticed signs
pointing to Ebbor Gorge and decided to investigate, finding
myself in magical thick woodland with trees of every description, plants, flowers, wild garlic. Suddenly I was plunging
down into a deep gorge, with rock towering on either side,
narrowing until it ejected me on to a hill where the view was

dominated by Glastonbury Tor in the distance. There was a sense of awe, wonder, peace, tranquillity, of being in sacred woodland, on holy ground, but as far as I know the place has never been a focus for religious ceremony or pilgrimage. And yet it was for me a very special place, where I experienced God as being very real and present. I reflected again on the way 'sacred space' can surprise us by suddenly appearing unexpectedly if we are open to experiencing it.

And so I came to Ammerdown, not knowing what to expect. I discovered one of the most diverse groups I have encountered. People of every sort of personality and theology, with an interest in the arts as Christians their only common factor and yet gelling in a remarkable way, tolerating each other as they hotly debated their understandings of sacred space. We were treated to a varied feast of input and experience. There were two lectures with slides, one looking widely at sacred space and sites ranging across the world, with pictures of mountains, parks and temples, the other showing how a gloomy chapel could be transformed into a welcoming, embracing sacred space using furnishings which harmonised with the nature seen from the window.

We had the opportunity to join in an early morning barefoot meditation, in which I found the initial strangeness rapidly becoming a deep inner experience as we walked in silence, connecting with the earth, finishing in the chapel for morning prayers, aspects of which felt intrusive after the stilling of the meditative walk. A woman who had left the rat race with her family to create an 'alternative' space in harmony with nature on a mountain in Wales shared honestly her experience and commitment to a different way of living. We had a session creating 'our' sacred space with elements from nature, wall hangings, drawings, sculptures, all generated spontaneously, coming to form a harmony out of diversity. This became our 'chapel' for a Catholic Eucharist leading the following morning into an Anglican one.

We shared in dances of universal peace, simple dances drawn from religious traditions with singing, in which we formed a circle, greeted and blessed one another, and worshipped in harmony of song and movement, creating another form of sacred space. We had a final session sharing insights but still debating about what makes for sacred space and what the role of artist is in helping to create it. One of the joys of the conference for me was one of those 'happen-chance' meetings. One of the organisers, Paul Middleton, had written a book about sacred space in India and I had sent off to him for a copy.[7] I introduced myself and we suddenly found ourselves chatting like old friends. When Sirpa met him at a later date she felt she had met up with someone she'd always known but hadn't seen for a couple of years, so out of the blue a friend had come naturally and easily into our lives.

I came away feeling that none of my questions had been 'answered', but reassured that others shared the questions passionately, and felt that the exploration of what sacred space is and how we create it is a critical one as we approach the end of the millennium. I also felt that the variety of activities and approaches we had engaged with said something about sacred space – it can't be approached from one angle or seen through one frame or reference. By its very nature it keeps defying single frames. The word, however, that did stay with me was the word 'connectedness' and specifically the connecting of earth and heaven. I had an increasing sense that what makes a space sacred is its ability to connect us deeply with ourselves, with the earth and cosmos that we are a part of, and with that which transcends the cosmos – the other, God, or that which the early Celts called the 'otherworld'.

And it struck me that part of what makes Glastonbury so powerful is the shape of the hill, reinforced by the tower which reaches up to the sky. As one stands on the top, one is aware of the dome of the sky all around. The earth seems to root one to the ground while the tower acts as a powerful connecting symbol, so that the energy flow is not only up from the earth but also down from the sky. This sense was reinforced for me the following day when I visited Burrow-bridge Mump, another rounded hill, with another ruined St Michael's church built on the top but more complete, and one of the churches said to form the St Michael line. It lies on the edge of the Somerset levels, one of the most important areas of wetland left in Britain, flooded in winter but rich meadow-land for grazing in summer. On the top I found myself drawn to prayer. The words seemed to come from outside me, and express the depth of desire I was beginning to experience. 'Lord, restore your earth to your people, and your people to your earth.' And then I found myself crying as I stood there feeling the energy of the earth coursing up through the soles of my feet into my body, while the other part of my mind saw the absurdity of this forty-five-year-old man on a Monday May Bank Holiday crouched in a corner of a church tower in the plains of Somerset, crying.

Prehistoric sites

On my way back from Ammerdown I visited the stone circle at Stanton Drew. It is badly signposted and hard to find, lying in a farmer's field. The farmer appears ambivalent about having such an attraction on his land and the notices demand-ing money are unfriendly. The first part one comes to is a group of stones called the Sanctuary which stand in the garden of a pub. Between the pub and the farmer's land with the circle on it is an old church which was locked, and the graveyard had a slightly spooky feel about it. I wanted to gain access so asked in the pub both where I would find the circle

and how I could get access to the church. The few locals were
very clear both that they knew who had the key and that they
were not going to let me know because 'It's Sunday afternoon
and the man may be resting and who wants to be knocked up
on a Sunday?' Once more I felt myself to be in a world far
removed from the bustle of city life where time took on a
different meaning and outsiders provided unwelcome in-
trusions. The circle itself, when you get to it, is a complex
series of large and small circles. There were sheep wandering
around the field and it had a desolate, uncared for feel.

The campsite was a different place on my return after the
weekend at Ammerdown. Where there had been space there
were now tents, caravans and trucks. I was curious about
these new neighbours but also resenting the invasion of what
had become 'my' space. It seems that personal space has a
sacredness about it which makes its invasion through rape
and mugging so heinous, and given that people's homes are
an extension of their personal space makes it difficult to
accept a concept of burglary as 'petty' crime. I was shocked at
how even the parking of someone else's car in the space where
I had previously parked mine sparked off resentment in me,
and recognised that the sort of hatreds that I had despaired
over when displayed in the war in the former Yugoslavia lay
not that far from the surface within me. The influx of campers
though also brought new encounters. That evening I met a
pair who spend their holidays visiting prehistoric sites
'because the atmosphere at them is so brilliant' and who
shared their experiences of Stonehenge, Avebury and other
sites with me. They both had brightly coloured hair and
appreciated the campsite 'because not everywhere accepts us'.

The following day I drove to Avebury, a massive prehistoric
complex. It consists of a huge stone circle, big enough to take
in part of the village built later and a main road which runs
through it; a long avenue of stones leading up to a prehistoric

site called the Sanctuary; one of the biggest prehistoric mounds in Europe, Silbury Hill; and a burial mound with several chambers, West Kennet Long Barrow. The church in the village was founded in about 1000 AD and has a particularly peaceful feel about it. The more I wandered around the area the more the place gradually took me over, especially when I walked along the avenue, imagining myself as part of a procession of people making their way towards the stone circle at one of the solstices for whatever ritual was to be enacted there, and when crouching in one of the burial chambers of the mound while a sharp shower spent itself outside. When I got back to my tent in the evening, I felt quite flat and low, feeling that my exploration was superficial, would add up to nothing and that I was wasting my time embarking on such a venture. I had had high expectations of Avebury, many people saying how much more atmospheric it was than Stonehenge, and felt let down by it. That seemed to say more about my mood than about the place itself, which alerted me to the subtle interaction between the power of places and the feelings with which we come to them.

The next morning I woke in a totally different frame of mind, alert, energised, alive. It turned out to be a magical day. I started by visiting Stonehenge, going with low expectations because several people had told me that it has lost its atmosphere through the number of tourists combined with people being kept away from the stones themselves. Instead, I felt strong energies from the stones even from a distance. I spent time sitting on the far side away from the car park and the streams of tourists, near a small burial mound, sensing the atmosphere and power of the place, and struck by a strong sense of the 'dome of the sky' all around. I went on to Old Sarum, an iron age fort, which later became the site of a Norman castle, palace and the original Salisbury Cathedral, feeling recharged as I walked around the ruins, taking in the

views over the city. A visit to Salisbury Cathedral itself followed. I was stilled by its awesome combination of simplicity,
space and scale.

I made for nearby Clearbury Ring, one of the points on the
ley line that many believe runs through Old Sarum and Salisbury. It lies some way from the nearest road. I was sure I had
spotted it and was about to set off confidently walking
briskly, but fortunately at that moment a local man came by
walking his dog in time to redirect me. As I climbed up
towards the thick clump of trees which clings to the top I
noticed a small group of people eagerly scanning the ground,
screeching with delight at intervals and calling excitedly to
each other. They turned out to be a group of botanists, ecstatic
at having found a rare orchid growing on its slopes, the 'burnt
orchid', a tiny plant which apparently only flowers after
fifteen years and even then not every year. It added to the
sense that I already had of being in a special place.

As I drove away I was forced to learn a painful lesson. I was
bowling along a deserted country road and thinking, 'At this
rate I'll be able to make Stourbridge while the restaurant is
still open and get some coffee and cake', when suddenly the
road in front of me was full of cows ambling along. I didn't
see any farmers with them, and wondered if they were on the
loose. I decided to gently nudge my way through them. To my
horror, they started stampeding ahead of me into another
field. I was about to drive on, but my way was blocked by a
burly and very irate farmer.

'What do you think you're doing?'

I started to stammer.

'Stampeding the cattle like that.'

'I wasn't, I was. . . .'

'You were stampeding the cattle in front of you. You
should know how to behave with cows. You should have
waited until they had all gone.'

Ruefully I realised that a few minutes before getting into the car I had been thinking of the Jains, who try to avoid killing any animal life, and regretting our Western speed which doesn't allow us that sort of respect for nature. And here I had been trying to push through a herd of cows, putting them at risk just to keep up with some artificial schedule I had created in my mind. There was only one thing to do.

'I apologise', I said.

I think he was a bit taken aback and he let me through. I drove on rather shaken by the incident.

From there I drove south to Knowlton Ring, which is one of the most outstanding examples of a Christian site on a prehistoric one – a ruined church stands in the centre of an earth henge which is reckoned to have been built for ritual purposes. Knowlton felt less atmospheric than I expected though there is something romantic about its situation, a long way from the nearest village, with the ancient church walls rising up from the midst of the henge.

My next visit to Stourhead Gardens was made purely out of curiosity, a desire to make good use of my National Trust membership and the call of coffee and cakes. To my delight I found it a place charged with energy from the variety of trees beautifully landscaped around lakes and streams. The redwood trees which stretch up endlessly until they lose themselves in the sky seemed particularly charged. My afternoon sleepiness was replaced by a renewed zest and awareness of the heart-stopping beauty around every corner. Suddenly I was in exactly the same sort of 'yurt' structure as in Glastonbury Abbey, also of stone but smaller, with a spring bubbling up on one side, and a window overlooking the lake on the other, through which I could see a crested grebe fishing. The place had a feel of perfection about it, and ecstasy seemed to bubble up inside me, matching the flowing waters which filled the air with their pure sounds. The words of Alexander Pope carved in the stone seemed particularly appropriate.

Nymph of the grot, these sacred springs I keep,
And to the murmur of these waters sleep.
Ah spare my slumbers; gently tread the cave
And drink in silence or in silence lave.

I drove on, singing joyfully. It was as though every place on this special day was bringing different delights. My final visit was to Cadbury Castle, a hill fort supposed to be the site of the legendary Camelot. The place sang in the evening light, adding to my deep sense of joy. At the bottom is St Thomas's Church which has the remains of a fourteenth-century painting, probably of St Thomas à Becket. As I stood by it I felt myself connected with saints through the ages and lifted into a different space. It felt like a perfect end to what had seemed a perfect day, a day of sheer gift, of delight after delight, a day where the light was clear and pure and I felt an inner clarity.

The next day I paid my last respects to Glastonbury. The following morning I discovered that I had had a nocturnal visitor – nearly all the chocolate biscuits which were in the outer part of the tent had been eaten. My route home took me via Kilpeck church near Hereford, renowned for its carvings. It is a tiny little twelfth-century church built on the site of an earlier Saxon church. The interior is small and very simple, with a plain wooden roof and the most extraordinary carvings imaginable inside and outside, some of which made me laugh out loud because of their exuberance, grotesqueness and humour. There were fantastic animals, a couple embracing, a dog partnered with a rabbit, someone playing a musical instrument, maybe a hundred carvings, nearly all in perfect condition, each absolutely full of character and life, displaying the extraordinary artistry. I kept on wandering around, allowing each fantastic carving to speak its unique message, until I could not take anything else in, and retreated to a nearby hillock, with ivy-covered walls, to be refreshed by its greenery.

And so eventually I arrived home from the first leg of my journey. I was astonished at how tired I felt. I could barely unpack, and the following day could do little more than sit around, as waves of deep exhaustion seemed to flow over me. But in no time I was gearing myself up for the most challenging leg of my journey – eight days totally on my own on an uninhabited island. I felt that I needed protection for the journey and Christian prayer and blessing. I decided to ring a woman colleague who, having been a deacon for many years, is now a priest. I had visions of myself kneeling while she made a sign of the cross over me and said a formal prayer. I should have known better, as she is someone who never does the expected. I arrived to find a massage table prepared. 'I thought I would massage your feet as a blessing for your journey,' she said. I found it a deeply moving experience, especially when she simply held each foot in turn before starting the massage. It also made me aware of tensions in other parts of my body. I felt very cared for in the process, but I still had fears and doubts and hesitations about what I was about to embark upon. How would I cope totally on my own for what seemed like for ever?

Notes

1. *Selected Poems*, Kathleen Raine, Golgonooza Press 1988, p67
2. *Pagan Religions of the Ancient British Isles – their nature and legacy*, Ronald Hutton, Blackwell 1991, cf p314–6
3. *A New View over Atlantis*, John Michell, Thames and Hudson 1983
4. *The Sun and the Serpent*, H Miller and P Broadhurst, Pendragon Press 1989
5. *The New Ley Hunter's Guide*, Paul Devereux, Gothic

Image 1994, p88
6. *The Celestine Prophecy*, J Redfield, Bantam 1994
7. *Adisthan: Sacred Space – Indian Christian Ventures*, Jyoti Saki and Paul Middleton, NBCLC, obtainable from Paul Middleton at 15, Evelyn House, Greatorex St., London E1 5NW

4

The Rhythm of the Island

For earth's days and nights are breaking over me,
The tides and sands are running through me.
Kathleen Raine[1]

The earth is filled with the Lord's unfailing love.
Psalm 33:5

Tuesday 6th June

Evening
I begin to feel despair as I set about packing for this next phase of the journey. Hammering at me is the knowledge that if I leave anything behind there will be no going back, no popping back to a shop. Once I am landed, and the boat has gone that will be it for eight days. There seems far too much stuff. I have to plan it exactly – what I need for the island, what for Findhorn, what for Orkney. It seems to take all day. I feel sick, and can feel a cold coming on, which I put down to fear; fear of what I am embarking on. I find it hard to say goodbye to Sirpa. I sense she will miss me a lot, and she has been feeling low. I sleep in the spare bedroom again as I am making an early start.

Wednesday 7th June

Morning

I sleep fitfully, wishing that I could train myself to sleep soundly before making a journey, instead of the restless tossing and turning I usually experience before I set off. It is a grey morning but dry. I make a detour to look at Long Meg and her Sisters, a stone circle in the Lake District, but am too tired to take much in. The drive through Scotland is beautiful, with the sunshine belying the cold wind. I stop for lunch by a waterfall but feel weak and a bit headachy.

Evening

I make Oban in good time. I have planned to spend the night there, but discover how difficult it is for a single person to find bed and breakfast accommodation. So many places which used to do single rooms have upgraded, the single rooms are now showers, and a double room would cost the double-room price. I begin to despair as I am directed to place after place to be told they have nothing available. Eventually I find a small, cramped, unappealing room with no washbasin. At least it is somewhere to lay my head, though a bit of me feels I would have done better sleeping in the car.

One of the many things which has been worrying away in my mind is how I will manage for a toilet on the island. I feel the need for a spade to dig a latrine with. I am relieved to find a garden shop open which has just what I need and I add it to the pile. I ring Sirpa to say a final 'Goodbye'. She asks if I am scared. I say, 'Yes'. I go for a walk. My legs are shaky. I feel sick with fear.

Thursday 8th June

Morning

I wake feeling more refreshed, with excitement alongside the fear. There is a strong wind blowing outside and I begin to worry about whether I will get on to the island. On my way to Luing I drive through unexpected scenery. It is very green and wooded, with the road winding through little hills with numerous pools, inlets and lakes. It's impossible to tell what is fresh or salt water. The road becomes narrower and narrower. I have a feeling of driving towards the edge of the world.

Arriving at the ferry across to Luing, there is fifteen minutes to wait. I feel excited, tense, nervous, tight muscles in my face, scared. Such a narrow strip of water, yet so powerful in stopping cars, and the complete dependence of the islanders on the little ferry. Luing appears as low, defined green hills with the occasional splash of rock; a few white houses with grey roofs and some mobile homes. Cold is seeping into my feet; seagulls are tossed by the wind but manage to soar on the currents. I have a nervous need for the toilet, feel fear, panic, trembling, tightening stomach. It's my last chance to turn back, to chicken out, not to go. I am very tempted but I don't give in. The ferry comes. I am on it and committed.

I arrive at the little village with its scattering of houses overlooking the sea. The wind hits me as I get out. The fisherman appears out of his house, short, bearded and in his fifties. He shakes my hand. 'Are you all set then?' I gulp, and say, 'Yes'. 'We can go whenever you're ready. Do you have much stuff?' I say that I have. He points out the boat and asks me to load up and give him a shout when I'm ready. I'm relieved when I see the boat – it's a substantial vessel, not the dinghy I had pictured. I ask him if I should settle up now. 'Noah,' he says. 'If I don't collect you, you won't owe me a penny.' A mental picture of myself starving but fifty pounds the richer comes into my mind, and I'm not sure whether to be grateful or not. In what seems no time we're racing across the water. I hardly have time to take the trip in, as I try to keep myself and my cases dry. The wind whips water over the bulwarks. Suddenly, there are the islands rising out of the sea. First a large one with a house on it, then the little one at the end, Holy Island itself. We draw into a tiny inlet which is totally still. There are steep rocks which I have a job scrambling on to. He hands my bags over, revs up the engine, and with a wave of his hand is gone. I am alone.

Afternoon
All I can focus on is the need to explore the island, to find a place to set up camp. I wander up and down through thick bushes and bog, constantly losing sight of the monastery, finding and losing paths until eventually I stumble across it – a mass of remains of buildings, with the chapel nearly complete, only missing its roof, and below it a little inlet with the well in between. I taste the water – it's beautifully fresh. I cast around, and eventually find a place up on the cliffs, out of sight of the monastery and sheltered by rocks from the north wind. I slowly and painfully drag the bags up step by step, stopping at one point to clean out of the bag a jar of pasta sauce which has smashed. It seems to be over everything, filling the bag with its smell, and leaving tiny splinters of glass everywhere.

Then comes the problem of pitching the tent on my own in a howling wind. I just get the groundsheet in place when the wind picks it up and puts it down topsy-turvy. The tent has to be aligned to it, but the peg won't go in one corner because it's rock and everything has to be moved. I eventually get one pole in, and then a second, but then there's a gust of wind and the whole thing collapses. Painstakingly I start again, and this time it holds for long enough to get the key pegs in. I inflate the bed, lie down for a delicious moment, but then feel the need to get the rest of the bags. I decide to walk barefoot – it feels like being a child again, and I have to be mindful of exactly where I'm putting my feet. It's the beginning of the process of slowing down. A bird chatters away at me as though in welcome. Little drops of light suddenly dance over the water and I feel such joy that I find myself bursting out into spontaneous applause.

My natural instinct is to go and ring Sirpa and say, 'I'm here, I'm fine, I've got the tent up, it's dry, I'm pleased to be here.' But, no phone; no contact. It is what I've chosen. I send her love through the ether and know she is thinking about me. And I become aware of the many for whom there is no one, no one with whom to share the silly everyday things as well as the deeper things, and I stay with them in prayer as best I can.

Evening
I feel as though I am as near heaven as one can get. I am sitting on a nature-made, grassy seat just behind my tent, looking down over a grassy slope with rocks either side, across rocks at the end, past a little lighthouse and out to sea. The sun is still high, bathing me with its warmth. I can't believe that I'm actually here on Holy Island, totally on my own, with a Celtic monastery and ruined chapel and underground store and holy well and a little graveyard where Columba's mother is said to be buried. I have a great sense of peace and the friendliness and acceptance of me by this place. I feel totally exhausted but unable to go to sleep with this amazing powerful light, and yet my body is crying out for rest.

There was a lamb lying in the monastery grounds which looked as though it was dying. I felt powerless to do anything, aware that it is part of nature's rhythm of birth and death but feeling a sadness.

I become aware of the vastness of the ocean around, with its ceaselessness, the water constantly moving.

Friday 9th June

Morning
A terrible night; no darkness! Light until well after eleven, light again at four, and in between a twilight. The half-light compounded by my fears – fears of falling, fears of being swept over the cliff by the wind, fears of the ground giving away beneath me, fears of sheep herding and crashing into me pushing me over the cliff, nameless fears and terrors. When I wake it's too cold to get up, so I snuggle into my sleeping bag and wait for the sun to reach the tent. In no time it's too warm to stay inside. It is calm. There is cloud but it is high cloud above; the sun is shining. I acknowledge the sun – its warmth, its power, its beauty, its ability to give sight and colour and quality of light, its enabling of life and its power to heal, its clarity. I give thanks for the gift of sight and, as I listen to the birds and the incessant murmuring of the sea, the gift of hearing. As I walk barefoot and feel the earth beneath me, holding me, sustaining me, meeting me with a firmness, strength, solidity, I give thanks for the earth. I go to the edge and begin to face the fear that my vertigo gives me – dizziness, my hands filling with sweat, my stomach churning and a fear of falling. I try to breathe into the fear. I sense this is important because behind this fear lies fear of people, fears of not being acceptable, not being good enough, and deeper than that a fundamental fear of trusting myself to life, to God, to people. And so I consciously give thanks for the gift of my life, my body, my being. I explore the area around the monastery.

The lamb is still alive, but appears to be dying. Near it is a tree, much of which is dead, but out of one part of it new leaves are growing – life out of death.

The monastery compound consists of a number of ruined buildings of differing dates. There are rough, stone steps leading up to it. Just inside, more steps lead down into a tiny cell, used for food storage. There is just room to clamber inside and put my hand on the shelf where hundreds of years ago I can imagine monks placing their precious supplies. The most substantial building is a simple, rectangular chapel, with the walls intact all the way round, but no roof. It was probably built in the tenth or eleventh century, replacing an earlier wooden one. By the entrance there is a small stone bench where I sit to meditate. The place is charged with prayerful atmosphere. There are other buildings, more recent – a possible mediaeval priest's house; a barn; an unusually shaped corn kiln like a rounded boat. Below the monastery is the well, behind which a spring bubbles up from the ground lying just above a little inlet, which is dry at low tide.

I sit in the chapel, imagining the monks praying there and wondering, 'What would they have worn? What would their relationships have been like?' I imagine them being in touch with the earth, the sky and sea, sensitive to the animal and bird life around and to every mood in the weather, smelling the rain before it arrives. Nearby are two beehive huts, one nearly complete. They are likely to have been built in the seventh century, shortly after the time of Columba. I marvel at the craftsmanship which has enabled these buildings to survive the winds and rain. It provides almost complete shelter, and I picture those early people huddled inside for protection.

Above the monastery my eye is taken up to another construction, a little graveyard with a simple cross etched into a rock. The grave is formed out of rough stones, laid in a circle. It is said to be the grave of Columba's mother, Eithne. It stands on a narrow ridge, overlooking the sea. I kneel by the rough cross and remember all our Celtic forebears, women and men who kept the faith alive through times of trial and difficulty.

As the wind rises, I watch a sheep going to the dying lamb, looking on helplessly as the lamb stretches up its head, bleats and then falls back, helplessly kicking its legs.

I return to the tent and I read Mother Julian.[2] I am struck by the simplicity and profundity of her vision of the hazelnut, which she sees as a symbol of the smallness of all created things before God. She writes that God made it, God loves it, God keeps it. I begin to look at everything on the island through her eyes. Of each thing I murmur, 'God made you, God loves you, God keeps you.' I begin to feel the truth of that for myself. 'God made me, God loves me, God keeps me.' And then she applies it to God – 'The Trinity is our Maker, our Keeper, our everlasting Lover' and adds 'The Trinity is our endless Joy and Bliss'.[3] I read Psalm 114:7,8: 'Earth, dance at the presence of the Lord, at the presence of the God of Jacob, who turned the rock into a pool of water, the flinty cliff into a welling spring'. As the psalmist addresses the earth as a living being, I am beginning to experience the island as a living being, nourishing me.

Afternoon
The lamb is still alive, twitching in the burning heat.

I explore the south end of the island. The lighthouse is an extraordinary feat of engineering, and I marvel at the courage of those who must have dragged each piece up here, constructing it in the teeth of the wind to provide this beacon of warning and hope. I am saddened by the litter, particularly the plastic bottles, lying around, disfiguring the landscape, a sign of human carelessness and disdain for God's creation. From here I can see how precarious my tent looks, clinging to a piece of cliff which overhangs the rocks below. No wonder I was fearful!

I pass the lamb on my way back. It was on its knees eating grass, but then would fall over, haul itself back on to its knees and continue munching, occasionally bleating piteously.

I discover a need to keep my tent tidy, and to look after my appearance. I regret not having a mirror to be able to check the cleanliness of my face. I feel more vulnerable than I thought, and am aware of the need to pay close attention to the state of perishable food, and the cleanliness of my washing-up brush. I am aware of my dependence on the well and on the elements. A hurricane would put me in real danger; even rain would totally alter my experience. And I become aware of how easy it would be to finish myself off, to walk over that cliff. Why go back? Why subject myself again to the pressures, the bills, demands, shoddy materialism, empty promises, and the constant racing just to keep in one place? I have broken all my ties to come here, so why not tidy the tent, and complete things by walking over the cliff?

As I go down to the well to fill my water bottle, I slip into the chapel and find myself drawn into intercessory prayer for those I know. I get back to the tent to discover that I have lost the top to the bottle. I go back down to the well – no sign of it. The moon is peeping through the cloud as I walk back. Suddenly, while my mind is miles away, I spot the top gleaming through the grass in the moonlight. I feel I have been led to it by God using the moon and give thanks. I only have the one bottle.

Saturday 10th June

Morning
Awake feeling very sexual. A grey, bleak-looking day. Reflect on the way the moment after sexual release can be a different kind of space (sacred space?). Decide to do everything today in silence – not thinking about this and that but focusing on breathing, being silent and being aware with as much of my being I can. I become aware of how much my mind chatters; how I try to eat my breakfast and look at the view at the same

time and miss aspects of both in the process. I reflect on the mystery of sexuality, the way sexual feelings are not there often when I want them to be, and then at other times come out of the blue, those times being the richest and most fulfilling and special.

I use a technique learned in 'Inner child' work of drawing with my left hand, and a spirit figure appears which I address in free written dialogue.

What are you?
I am your spirit: I am your imagination, your hopes, your fears, your desires, your passions. I watch over you, care for you, warn you when I see you damaging yourself but often you will not, do not listen.

Where are you?
I am within you and without you, above you, below you, around you. I am the 'is-ness' which is you. I have always been there, part of you from before you were born, and I will be part of you and apart from you as you die.

How can I listen more?
You must still yourself, still your mind, become silent.

When?
Always. Tomorrow arises out of today. The future is in the now. The past is in the now. Now is the day of the Lord, the day of salvation. You only live now, here, in this moment, in this body, on this earth, loved and kept by this God, this being who is light and dark, day and night, being and not being, three and one, whole and parts, spirit and non-spirit, all things and nothing, in everything and in nothing. Walk in your spirit. That is *the* way, there is no other.

What about Jesus?
Jesus walked in the way. Jesus is the way. Jesus lived as the way. Jesus is the Christ who is God and is not God, who is in everything and in nothing. Jesus is the focus of all life, all living which is being born, living now, dying, rising. There is

nothing else. To be united with Christ is to live the way: there is no other.

What about Buddha, Muhammad?

They lived the way. Christ *is* the way. They show the way. Christ *is* the way. They manifest aspects of the way. Christ *is* the way.

Where is God to be found?

In living the way; in living as Christ lived. Not in a book, not in teaching, not in worship, but in living the way. The height of worship is the centre of living the way; the desire to worship is a longing for living the way; the poverty of worship is our poverty in living the way.

As I read back what I have written, I am astonished at what has come up from my subconscious. It is as though the words have come from deep within me and from outside. They make sense to me, sense of my experience of receiving wisdom I believe to be of God from many sources and yet feeling that Christ is the centre of all; a sense of Jesus Christ being the way, the truth and the life, not exclusively but inclusively.

I then read in Mother Julian. 'And after this I saw God in a point ... by which vision I understood that he is in all things.'⁴ ... 'See I am God. See I am in everything. See, I do everything. See, I never lift my hands from my works, nor ever shall, without end. See, I lead everything to the end I ordained for it from without beginning, by the same Power, Wisdom and Love with which I made it.'⁵ I feel sadness at the sinfulness of my blindness to the simplicity of 'God is in everything' through most of my life, and am encouraged that the next 'shewing' of Mother Julian is about Christ's blood washing us from sin.

Afternoon

I feel so much safer here now, trusting the place and the tent. ... I enjoyed a 'cooked lunch' today. To the apple and banana of yesterday I added chicken soup, decaf coffee and two bourbon biscuits. One of the most enjoyable meals I can remember. ... I feel as though the cries of the birds have become the call of friends.

Early evening
Don't remember ever feeling such a strong sense of sin. Came back from collecting litter – seven or eight sackfuls of plastic from one area. I put them in a wet cave with beautiful mosses and primroses and wild garlic at the entrance. To clear one area I had to do sacrilege to another. I am deeply conscious of my careless use of plastic, and the speed with which the human race is littering the planet, and my lack of awareness, mindfulness of God being in all things. A deep sense of need for reassurance of God's love, and the washing in the blood of the Lamb. As I have had to face, a dying lamb is not a pretty sight.

Late evening
I have been crying. I read Hopkins' 'The Grandeur of God' and found the last two lines moving me to tears. Nature is never spent, he says,

> *Because the Holy Ghost over the bent*
> *World broods with warm breast and with ah! bright wings.*[6]

Sunday 11th June

Morning
Slept badly. Woke up early – couldn't get back to sleep. Headache over one eye – like the beginning of a 'wipe out' day at home, but here there are no external pressures so it is coming from me. Decided not to take painkillers. Bitterly cold

morning with the northerly winds strong, but clear sky and sharp views. Headache better after breakfast. Prayer read in *Carmina Gadelica* seems very fitting:

> And as the mist scatters on the crest of the hills
> May each ill haze clear from my soul, O God.[7]

Mother Julian's vision that 'All shall be well, and all shall be well, and all manner of things shall be well' begins to make sense.[8] She was writing against the background of wars, the plague and natural disasters. She states that we don't need to know *what* will be well, or *how* it will be, but only believe *that* all will be well. The one thing we can be sure of is that when we see everything clearly in the light of God, none of us will be able to say, 'If only that had not happened all would have been well'. In the light of God's love, we will see that everything has been well. The only power sin has over us is to increase the honour God gives us because of his love for us. But that is not an excuse for sin because the more we see and accept God's love at the heart of the universe, the more we naturally loathe everything that stands against all being well.

Afternoon
The wind has dropped, the air is cool, the sun is deliciously warm and there is an afternoon stillness in the air as the birds lazily soar. I feel the stillness all around. Even in the sea there is a stillness, a stillness in the grandeur of the mountains of Mull across the water, a stillness in the island, a stillness within me. And a sense that all of it is made, loved and kept by God. To pray words would be superfluous at this moment. In this state, being itself is prayer, is being held in the love of God.

The lamb is dead. Already the eyes have been plucked out.

Evening
As I walk back from fetching water the moon appears

through the clouds, a full moon. I return to the tent, put on sweater and woolly hat and lie with my torso out of the door-way, watching the moon rise in the east and the sun setting in the west.

Sunset; Moonrise;
The one disappearing, waning, the other rising, waxing.
The one in death lighting the other in life.
The one scattering its last shreds of glory,
The other clear, true, of one purpose.
The one merging into orange rays, the other perfect in
    circularity.
The one strange, dangerous, unseeable, the other lovingly
    reflecting earth.
The one now beating, now caressing, now burning, now
    reviving,
The other sure and true and constant.
The one bringing life, the other ecstasy and wonder.
The one knowable to all, the other mysterious and elusive.
The one lighting the world, the other a path for the lost.
The one never changing, the other constant in variety.
The one before whose power to lie, the other before whose
    grace to dance.

Monday 12th June

Morning
Woke up in the early hours. It was so light! Went to the loo. Full moon shining on the tent; sunrise in the east. Got up at eight. A softer, gentler wind – warmth in the air. In prayer in touch with a deep yearning, longing for all to be well. A sense of the pain and grief of sin, my sin and the world's sin, and the hurting of the earth, and Jesus the one who cleanses sin and shows how all shall be well. I reflect on the sun and the

moon, and become aware of how my life has been like the sun, trying to see everything, know everything, understand everything, and how different the moon is with its coming and going, and its single-minded clear localised purpose and I long for the beauty of that clarity in my life. I notice how tense I feel at times – not so very different from when I am at work, so the stress is coming from me rather than from the external world.

I begin to appreciate what Sister June meant when I asked her advice about patterns for my days on the island, and she said, 'Listen to its rhythm.' It feels like a subtle combination of the natural process of day and night (sunrise, morning, noontide, afternoon, evening, twilight, sunset, moonrise) with the weather and with the tides adding their subtle rhythm which shifts a little each day. I find myself falling into a way of being where my rhythm is determined by my body in harmony with nature, not by any clock. I 'observe' time rather than letting it dictate to me.

Mother Julian:
Truth perceives God
and Wisdom contemplates God,
and from these comes the third,
and that is a holy, wonderful delight in God, which is love.[9]

Midday
Now the wind has dropped to a whisper, the sea is calm, the sun is hot. I only meditate for twenty minutes because I find myself caught up in the nature around – the seagulls flying over; the sheep grazing; a lamb staring at me; the fishing boat drifting lazily past; the bee flying over; the sea, land, sky, all interconnected, all held, sustained, loved and created by God.

Mid-afternoon
South-east coast of the island. I have just seen my first seal,

gently bobbing above the water and then effortlessly disappearing underneath. Sea birds are whirling overhead, two large ducks are swimming across the bay, a cormorant stands on the rock in the distance. I pass the cave where I had piled what seemed to be an enormous heap of plastic litter, and it looks so small now in proportion to the enormity and timelessness of the rocks towering above the cave. 'All shall be well, and all shall be well and all manner of things shall be well.'

Late afternoon

I feel the island beginning to take me over, lulling me, holding me, nurturing me; as though I am melting into it, becoming part of it. I fear that I will be unable or unwilling to leave. I have discovered a new delight. When my face is grubby, instead of using 'wet ones', I rub it on the fresh, cool grass, smelling the earth and feeling it envelop and cleanse me. Perhaps I should have been born a sheep! I prepare my evening meal of noodles with pasta sauce, cheese, peppers, spring onion, baked beans and a spoonful of garlic pickle. I have the same every evening, rejoicing in its simplicity and deliciousness.

Evening

This evening is unutterably magical. The sun is setting over Mull, just the last whisper of it disappearing below the hills. Above it, a delicate orange merging into azure blue wisps of cloud, tinged with pink and gold. The mountains of Mull standing out silhouetted against the sky. The sea totally calm. The moon, full moon, rising in the east. I have seldom seen it looking so clear, a delicate yellow like the globe of a gas street light, glowing faintly. Its shadows look like a map of the countries of the world, as though it is mirroring the earth, hanging in the sky, perfect in its roundness, beautiful in its clarity. Gradually it creates a single line of golden light reaching across the water, touching the island at the point where the monastery lies. It is as though the moon is greeting the monastery and the monastery is greeting the moon. Now, where the sun is setting, more clouds, glorious in bright orange, filling the sky, deepening in the distance into a deep pink, and further above tiny, tiny, thin cloud tinged with light pink, like angels' wings, reach up through the sky. It is as though heaven and earth are connected and all are one, and there is no division and no separation, and only unity and God is all and is in all. It's as though I am one with all of this, part of all of this. I can feel the energy of the earth beneath my feet rising up through me. I am not separate from what I see, I am part of what I see, and what I see is part of me and we are one, as the earth and heaven are one. I feel beautiful, I feel beauty, I feel a fullness, wholeness, a one-ness.

When I go to zip up the tent the moon is shining on me. I step out. I see a delicate thin light detaching itself from it and coming towards me like a spirit. The moon has a halo around it. The sea looks like glass, as though one could walk on it. Suddenly, magically, over the surface of the sea, lights appear floating; beautiful shining lights. As they get nearer I see that it is a cruise ship quietly making its way up the sound.

Tuesday 13th June

Morning
I have nightmares during the night. About being back at work – confusing instructions, people angry; about a weird art exhibition where I am chased by a huge insect and find my car has been crushed, but where I meet a friendly woman with children.

As I lie in bed I find myself giving thanks for all the people who have touched my life. They appear in my mind like a procession of precious jewels. A phrase from Mother Julian strikes me. 'In the taking of our human nature Jesus restored life to us, and in his blessed dying upon the cross, He birthed us into endless life.'[10] I feel that life all around me and within me. She sees the three key properties of God as being life, love and light. She asks: What is the Lord's meaning? 'Love was his meaning. Who showed it thee? Love. What showed he thee? Love. Why did he show it thee? For love.'[11] I experience the island bathing me in that love. I reflect on the dreams and feel they are pointing to two worlds I live in. In one, I feel at home and know my way around, but push responsibility away. In the other, I take responsibility, but I am frightened and don't know my way around; I feel trapped and yet in that world is the feminine and creativity, and it is that world I want to explore.

When I open my eyes after meditation, it is as though I am seeing the world for the first time.

The silence is disturbed by a military ship, its engine aggressive, menacing. I remind myself that although their purpose is evil the machines and the pilots have been conceived in love.

Afternoon

I am in a slight state of shock and trembling from having met another person. Occasionally yachts put in, people go and look at the monastery, and sail away. So far I have been undisturbed by other humans. This afternoon there were no yachts. I was sitting by the well, when I thought I heard voices. Soon it was clear they were voices. As I sat there, in the hollow, a man appeared. He explained that he was with a group of youngsters from a nearby outdoor centre who had canoed over to bivvy overnight. I explained my purpose there. There were a few moments of comfortable silence and then he said, 'Well, I'll leave you to your solitude.' I felt he understood and that I will not be disturbed. It still felt something of a shock though.

Late evening
I go down to get water. In spite of the cloud there is a very special quality of light. I stand on Eithne's grave and feel moved by the sense of those who kept the faith alive in all weathers, battling against the elements in places like these. I slip into the chapel on my way back and am immediately enveloped in an atmosphere of stillness, prayerfulness and peacefulness. I pray at length – the prayer is drawn out of me. As I am about to turn in, the sun appears below the cloud, warming me with its heat, bathing the sea in a stairway of glittering, dancing gold. I mockingly curse its beauty which will not allow me to go into the tent, feeling it would be sinful to leave it. Reluctantly I tear myself away to give my body the rest it cries out for.

Wednesday 14th June

Morning
A sudden change in the weather from cool and dry, to scorching hot. Suddenly from having been living in the tent with forays outside, I find myself living outside with forays in. I become aware for the first time of the connection between a deep sense of God's love at the heart of everything and a sense of sin. The more I am aware of love, the more horrendous everything which is not of love seems. I had always thought of sin as contrasted with God's holiness, and I had struggled with that, because holiness to me felt harsh, unrelenting and cold, whereas there has been a warmth and acceptance about sinfulness. But now I experience love at the heart of everything, I feel a sense of horror of everything which is against love, against all being well, and all manner of things being well which lies in me and in the world. Suddenly I have a new sense of the need for cleansing, washing, confession, renewing and the role of the blood of Jesus, again something I had

struggled with before, seeing it as a barbaric sacrifice dressed up to look all right because it was God doing it. I read Psalm 118 with its powerful refrain: 'For his love endures for ever.'

I begin to reflect on my life, on its messiness, on the race to keep up, on the superficiality with which I do so much, on my need to try to encompass everything, and yet the constant feedback that somehow my presence enables others, and I long to have a sense of God's purposes for me. I begin to feel I can trust him to show me in his time. I begin to offer every part of my being to God, and I find myself stretching my arms and legs up like a child reaching up for a hug, and allow a deep sense of God's love to embrace my body. The wind turns the pages of my Bible to Psalm 148, calling on the whole earth to praise the Lord because 'his name is high above all others' (v 13). And I feel it is enough to stay with that sense of God whom I can trust, who is love, who is more than the nature all around, which is in itself so worthy of all my praise and worship.

Mid-afternoon

I go down to the south end of the island and cross the bog. Suddenly, it is as though I am seeing the island for the first time. It is teeming with life: flowers, blue, purple, pink, red, yellow, white and insects, butterflies, moths, flies of every shape and hue. I feel as though the whole island is pulsing and vibrating with life. I wander delightfully through the bogs and round the edge of the cliffs. Scene after scene transfixes me – a pool teeming with tadpoles; furry white plants, soft and gentle to the touch like fine nylon; a spider's web shimmering in the sunlight; a cave full of wild garlic; a rock covered with moss as soft as velvet; fresh light green ivy growing up a rock face; tiny red flowers clinging to the surface of a stone. Wherever I look there is a buzz and variety of life, and I find myself glorying in it, enjoying every glance, lost in a magical world, feeling that the only intruder is me. I have a deep sense of the love of God expressed through the nature of which I am part, and a sense of beginning actually to trust that for the first time. And I reflect that that variety and bursting of life was found not so much in the centre of the island, but on the margins, in the bogland, the apparent wasteland, the neglected parts.

Evening
The lamb is more or less unrecognisable now, much of it having been eaten away. From being the live animal that I first saw, it has become a twisted pile of wool and skin and bone. I am reminded of the bodies in Burundi and Rwanda and so many other parts of our world.

I call into the chapel, but don't feel any of the atmosphere I felt the previous evening.

Called into chapel later in the evening – felt the atmosphere again; prayer drawn out of me.

Thursday 15th June

Terrible night; very restless; tense, jumpy legs; night seemed to go on for ever; extremely windy, whole tent straining and shaken.

Dream about being lost in New York without a map. Not enough money to buy one. Eventually find my own way back to the hotel, even directing some others in the process. I don't have my own identity, not even my own name in this alien world and yet I survive. Perhaps there is hope for me in this new unfamiliar world that I am entering.

Read Proverbs 3:5: 'Put all your trust in the Lord, and do not rely on your own understanding.' Sense that we can only trust what we love, and we can only love what we experience. For me it has been the experience of nature here which has enabled me to experience the love of God.

Early evening

I feel exhausted and a whole mixture of feelings about going back to the mainland tomorrow and on towards Findhorn. Very sad to leave the island, which I feel I am only just beginning to get to know. I have been wandering around re-sensing the beauty, feeling the sadness of leaving, but already having left a little, so the looking has become unseeing, as though I don't dare really to see it now because the pain of leaving would be too hard.

Then there is the feeling of wanting to re-connect with people. I find myself fantasizing that someone I know will be on the boat with the fisherman. Then there are fears. Perhaps something has happened to one of the family. Then the question, 'What's happening in the world?' The concerns of the world still feel very distant. The island has a quality of timelessness about it, which puts the daily world of politics, and even the agony of war, into perspective. But it will only remain timeless as long as we take steps to stop the polluting of our planet.

Then there are the regrets: not enough time spent meditating or appreciating the island or reading; no clear 'vision' for the future; no deep insights, only simple ones gleaned from others.

And so the day has been about beginning to let go, clearing up, packing, and wrestling with bushes to clear a path to the rocks.

10.30

Last walk. Spent time in the beehive hut as the earliest connection with the Celtic saints. Didn't know how to give thanks and appreciate all the time has meant to me but prayed as best I could. Final prayer in the chapel. Aware as I walk back to the tent of how much more there is of the island and its nature to observe and learn from – feels a good note to leave on. I feel a sense of achievement as I get back to the tent. I've made it here and it's been very good, and I've lived very well here.

Friday 16th June

Relieved to find that it was dry though cloudy when I woke up. Very mild, almost muggy. No wind. Take two bags down to the rocks. Shocked at how long it takes. Quickly back and pack up the tent. Say farewell to the site, sad to be leaving, anxious about whether the fisherman will come, excited about going. Walk down, saying goodbye to the various places as I pass them.

I make it only minutes before the time we agreed. I sit, absorbing the calmness of the sea and the mildness of the air. I feel a mixture of strong emotions: grief and joy, mixed with the physical exhaustion from dragging my bags down. A boat appears, disappears – I confidently wait for it to reappear in the bay; it doesn't and I see it carry on past the island. I wait. Another boat appears, comes nearer – this is it! The fisherman and a woman, his wife, a taller woman with hands crippled by disease. He gives a friendly wave, and moments later is alongside. He had had an oil leak, and his wife had to come holding a pipe in place. In spite of that he was only twenty minutes behind the time we'd agreed. Within seconds my gear was aboard, I had hopped in and we were steaming away. I stared back at the island – nothing distinctive about it, nothing to make one look twice – and yet it had given me so much. Soon it was out of sight; other islands, seals, more islands and then Cullipool. In no time my bags and I were on dry land, he was off helping his sons unload their boat, and I was drinking coffee in their kitchen while his wife shared her sense that the island has more atmosphere than Iona.

I ring Sirpa before catching the ferry. She sounds well and

happy. 'How can you be tired after a week on your own?' How do I begin to explain? 'Were you lonely?' 'No.' 'Did you talk to yourself?' 'No, mainly on paper.' Life much the same for her – work, paper work, violence in the city. I talk with Nina – good to hear her voice. I feel that it will be difficult to re-connect after this period. I feel as though I have changed, and we will both have adjusted to living on our own. The day feels like a transition day, getting used to the radio and news, in which little seems to have changed; listening to music; anxious about fixing up a bed and breakfast place to stay; enjoying driving again, not really taking in the scenery, bemused by the crowds of people in Inverness, taken aback by the sensuality of younger women that I see.

7.00
Major frustration! I am in a 'bed and breakfast'. The one luxury I have looked forward to is a soak in a hot bath and a hair wash. AND THERE IS NO HOT WATER!

9.00
I am washed and cleansed and shaved! I went for a walk – wonderful, ancient woodland with cedars, yews and strange looking trees. I lean my palms against them and feel different types of energy coming off them. There is a little boggy area which reminds me of the island, and I feel renewed and refreshed by nature. On my return I find that the water is hot so I soak in a hot shower. On the island I had used Wet Ones to wash with each morning, and felt remarkably clean. As I use an electric razor I hadn't shaved, so shaving was quite painful.

Sink gratefully into bed.

I sleep well. Woke feeling a bit sick as though I had had rather too much sleep. I am the only guest in the hotel, so eat a solitary breakfast. I feel ready for Findhorn – open to whatever the experience brings but also nervous. . . .

Notes

1. *Selected Poems*, Kathleen Raine, Golgonooza Press, p22
2. *A Lesson of Love: The Revelations of Julian of Norwich*, ed/trans Father John-Julian OJN, DLT 1988
3. ibid, p9
4. ibid, p29
5. ibid, p32
6. *Poems and Prose of Gerard Manley Hopkins*, sel W H Gardner, Penguin 1953, p27
7. *Carmina Gadelica*, Alexander Carmichael, Floris Books 1992, p198
8. *A Lesson of Love: The Revelations of Julian of Norwich*, ed/trans Father John-Julian OJN, DLT 1988, p62
9. ibid, p100
10. ibid, p166
11. ibid, p213

Midsummer Magic

Because I love
The summer air quivers with a thousand wings,
Myriads of jewelled eyes burn in the light.
Kathleen Raine[1]

He who travels far will often see things
Far removed from what he believed was Truth.
Herman Hesse[2]

Many waters cannot quench love, no flood can
sweep it away.
Song of Songs 8:7

Findhorn

I had hesitated for some years before going to Findhorn. It was a name that had cropped up on various occasions. Then a friend lent Sirpa a book called *Flight into Freedom*.[3] Sirpa passed it on to me. I found it utterly fascinating and deeply disturbing. It was the autobiography of Eileen Caddy, telling of how her husband, Peter, was made redundant and they ended up living in a small caravan near a rubbish dump on some sands by the Moray Firth. Previously she had been through some horrendous experiences, but during this time had begun to receive messages from 'an inner voice'. When

she trusted them and followed them, everything they pre-
dicted happened. Peter also began to trust in her messages,
and together they followed the voice, even when it seemed to
be leading them nowhere. They were joined by a woman
called Dorothy Maclean, who had a gift for listening to
nature spirits. With the instructions from Dorothy and
Eileen's 'voice' Peter began to develop a vegetable garden on
the barren soil, which grew vegetables of extraordinary size
and flavour, such that botanists and the press began to be
interested. As people heard about the garden they were
attracted to come and join in what they felt was happening,
and so the community started. Peter's underlying principle
was that work is love, not something you do so that you can
then relax, or have enough to live on, but something you do
for its own sake. The community was therefore based on the
principle of work as love, and Peter did not tolerate hangers
on. Following the guidance given through Eileen's 'voice', the
community continued to grow and grow, eventually buying
the nearby hotel from which Peter had been made redundant.
The community has developed through ups and downs; it is
now thirty-three years old, and has about two hundred and
fifty members, with about three hundred associates living in
the area. Thousands of people visit every year and take part in
a wide variety of courses and workshops.

What both Sirpa and I found disturbing was the fact that
Eileen believed her inner voice to come from Christ. She was
clearly a person of total integrity and committed love, who
seemed to be in touch with something supernatural that was
wholly good. If a test of prophecy is its ability to predict the
future accurately then her voices were true; if a test is the fruit
of the Spirit and qualities of love, joy and peace, then that
shone through. And yet the whole philosophy didn't fit with
traditional Christian teaching. The community sees itself as
being a centre of light among other centres of light, who are

held together by beaming love and light into the world bringing forward a new age of a healed world and earth. There
were also other difficult elements from a Christian perspective, in that Eileen had left her husband and children to marry
Peter, and later on in life Peter left her to marry a younger
woman. And yet there was something in her writing which
rang true.

I was visiting therefore with hesitations, having had to
pluck up my courage to decide to go. I was curious about the
community, wary of it, but prepared to be open to what it
might have to offer. I wanted to visit a place experienced as
being sacred by many but which has only become a focus in
the past few decades. I wanted to be somewhere where midsummer was celebrated in style. I was also looking forward to
a week of sacred dance which is also known as circle dance.
Sacred dance is a simple form of dance to traditional folk
music from European countries. The dances are generally
danced in a circle, with hand contact and repetitive movements, so that an atmosphere of stillness and unity within the
group builds up. Because they are simple and repetitive they
can be done by anyone no matter how clumsy they feel themselves to be. What makes them different from folk dances is
the spirit and atmosphere in which they are danced. They are
undertaken mindfully; there is always a central focus of a
candle, sometimes surrounded by flowers and leaves, or
scarves; time is spent in quietness at the beginning to connect
with the other participants and with the earth. There is something very simple and yet very powerful and absorbing about
them. In the circle there is no heirachy; everyone is in their
own space but connected to everyone else; the space in the
middle seems to fill with energy; frequently as the dance ends
there is a magical moment where people are still, absorbing
the powerful energy which has been developed. People are
encouraged to channel the energy as healing for themselves,

all humanity and the earth. Each time I participate I feel a
sense of being part of a great whole, being held, being at one,
not just with the individuals in the circle, but in a mysterious
way with the earth, the universe and all humanity.

My most powerful experience of sacred dance was a day of
dancing the St Francis canticle of creation in Liverpool
Cathedral. We spent most of the day downstairs going
through the dance and then went up into the body of the
cathedral to dance it. As I write, I can feel the power of
emotion in my stomach that I experienced, a mixture of vul-
nerability, tearfulness and joy. It was as though suddenly all
sorts of bits of myself, my spirituality, my faith, my feelings,
my body, my mind, my beliefs all came together with the
prayer about sun, moon, stars, about the four elements of
earth, fire, water and air, interwoven with the redemption
through Christ and life coming through death. And through
the dance I was able to enter into that, experience that, with
the whole of myself. I could be the fire, sizzling; I could be the
water, flowing; I could pound the earth and call up its power;
I could be the air, light and floating; I could enter the depths
of hell sinking into the centre of the spiral, and I could experience the resurrection coming out of the darkness into light
and joy and free dance. And I could do that surrounded by a
group of people, held by them, providing a container for a
depth of emotion I have rarely experienced and would not
have known how to contain on my own. It was, for me, an
experience of sacred space – creating a humanly sacred space
in the huge empty space of the cathedral, investing it with an
energy that somehow seemed to connect earth and heaven
and humanity in one.

So I was prepared to put up with what I expected to be a
weird, way out, esoteric, potentially dangerous community in
order to have the experience of sacred dance. I knew that I
could never repeat the sort of experience I had had in the

cathedral, but I was hoping that some of the same elements would be present. I was therefore totally unprepared for the experience that awaited me. The word which comes as I reflect on that week is 'Gift'. It was as though the whole week, every event, every encounter, every second was sheer, sheer, unexpected gift. It was as though I had come home in the deepest possible sense, and for the first time experienced myself living out of my innermost being in a harmony of body, mind and spirit, acting out of the depths of who God has created me to be. In the process I discovered an inner beauty in people, in everything around me and, most startling of all, an inner beauty in myself, as though experiencing myself for the first time as created in God's image, deeply loved and precious to God. The more I opened myself up to the experience of the week, the more it felt I was being given. At one point, I felt so full, that I started to pray, 'Please, no more God, no more. I can't contain any more of this fullness and giftedness.' But then, as soon as I realised what I was saying I prayed: 'No, Lord, if you've got more for me then I want whatever you want to give me.'

A special place

So, what was it about the week? The first thing I was aware of was the atmosphere. I felt it particularly in two places, the first being the original garden where the vegetables were grown, which is kept as a sanctuary garden. It was difficult to imagine it as a rubbish dump on rough sands because now it is rich in vegetation and trees, and has a deeply powerful atmosphere. 'Why here of all places?' I wondered. I guess Moses may have felt the same when faced with the burning bush. The second was the nature sanctuary which has been built into a quiet garden in another part of the grounds. Again the tiny round building repeats the yurt shape I had met before, but specifically designed as a place for meditation and quiet. I was unable to walk into it without feeling a deep sense of calm and inner stillness and connectedness. On the first day those who were new to the place went on the daily tour for visitors. It was in the nature sanctuary that the person leading the tour shared the strangeness many experience at seeing community members there hugging each other. He talked very simply about the importance of not bottling up emotions, especially for men. It was as though he sensed that a group of strangers, many curious day-trippers, would feel safe enough to receive that level of sharing in such a sacred atmosphere. These places were in addition to the sanctuary, where people meet to meditate twice a day and which is always open for prayer and meditation, in itself a very special place.

Then there were the members of the community. I was struck at how ordinary, balanced and sane they seemed; very different from one another, with a wide mix of nationalities, and deeply accepting of different spiritualities and traditions. They also seemed to have the gift of not taking themselves too seriously – deeply committed to what they were seeking to do and be, and what they believe the community stands for – but all too aware of their humanity and failings. Looking around in the evenings, when the thirty or so of us on the week were joined by a hundred or more community members, I several times felt that I had never seen so many 'beautiful people' gathered in one place. At the same time, far from being 'heads in the clouds' people, I found a community which is putting belief into practice in very practical ways. They are at the forefront of developing ecological housing and alternative means of generating power in this country, and organise international conferences on ecology, bringing together experts in a wide variety of fields. Johnathan Porrit and Prince Charles have both been speakers at a recent conference.

Then there was the expression of their values in everything that was done. Their philosophy is that things are only worth doing if they are done well, with the utmost love, care and attention. Love must never be sacrificed to efficiency or haste, so if it takes more people, or seems less economic, that is less important than the spirit in which things are done. I experienced the effect of that in every part – the cleanliness of the place, the quality of the food, the fresh, beautifully arranged flowers on the tables, the professionalism and care taken by the workshop leaders. Every aspect of the place seemed to reflect their underlying love commitment.

Then there was the experience of the circle dancing. I hadn't realised that it was to Findhorn that Professor Bernard Wosien had first taken the dances he collected to see if they could use them, and that Findhorn is the focus and centre for Circle Dance worldwide. The quality of the dancing I had already done seemed to pale into nothing in comparison with the depth of spirituality, care and skill with which the dances were taught and led. In the afternoons we had a choice of singing, playing or dancing, and I opted for dancing. We worked with twelve dances through the week, some more complex, many of which I was convinced over the first couple of days that I would never master. To my surprise and delight I found that suddenly during the week the dances seemed to be in my body, and I was able to relax, not worry about what to move when, and totally give myself over to them.

But it was spiritually that I found the most surprising thing happening. In spite of my wariness I found that I felt spiritually in tune with so many of the people I met and talked with. It was partly to do with their acceptance of the importance of nature, and the natural way in which they seemed to connect with creation and the earth. But, more than that, it felt that so many of the values they were expressing and living by were ones that lay at the heart of my Christian longing, but which

I so seldom experienced expressed in myself or Christian churches and communities. It was as though even when theologically I found myself differing from people at a deeper level, I was in tune spiritually with them. But at the same time I felt something missing in my first few days there, which led to a feeling of alienation.

A Christian presence

On the Sunday morning I was astonished to see 'Taizé' as the morning session. Taizé is a monastic community in France which has been an astonishing focus, particularly for young people, and has produced simple liturgies and chants which have found their way into churches all over the world. We went to a nearby building called Minton House, which over-looks the bay. We crowded into the 'ballroom', a large room with a wide curved bay window and wooden floor, for what I experienced as being one of the most deeply worshipful services I have been at. We started with silence and then sang a Taizé 'Sanctus' in three parts walking around. Then we did simple movements to a 'Kyrie Eleison'. That was followed by an extended singing of an 'Alleluia', during which people were invited to come into the middle where there were candles burning, to pray silently and meditate. I found that experience particularly deeply moving. A reading followed, after which a woman played a Celtic harp and sang a haunting melody. The final corporate act was to sing part of a Celtic blessing to each other with simple movements as we moved round the room, and we were dismissed with the whole blessing being said. My unease, however, was with what was said to accompany the singing which put the stress on singing to the God within us, and the light within us. It was as though the leaders were deliberately excluding the Christian content from the deeply Christian songs. The reading was from 'White Eagle' and struck me as being very dualistic about light transforming matter and looking to a future time when we would rise above matter. It left me feeling alienated and very alone. It was as though I had arrived somewhere where I felt so at home and yet where there was no place for me with my Christian faith and rootedness. The feeling of aloneness was reinforced by sharing in a community wedding afterwards, a joyful, exuberant celebration, and suddenly feeling an aching deep inner loneliness, aware of Sirpa not sharing the experience with me, aware that some aspects of it would be alien to her (she 'hates' circle dancing!) and aware of all the levels on which we don't connect or get things together as well as the many in which we do. What made the experience different for me was that although previously I would have continued to join in and pretended to be happy, this time I took myself off. Feeling that I hadn't got to know anyone well enough yet to share the experience, I allowed myself to feel the aloneness without wallowing in it.

Later that day I happened to glance at a leaflet I had picked up when in Minton House. In it I saw that far from being part of the Findhorn Foundation, Minton House is a Christian centre committed to inter-faith dialogue and building links between the Christian churches and Findhorn! I arranged to meet the Director, Judith Meynell, a dynamic, upper class woman, who owns the house, and had moved up some years ago looking for something she wasn't finding in the Church at the time. She had felt a rootedness of faith lacking in the Foundation – it was as though people were so keen to be open to all faiths that they didn't allow themselves to tap into the depth, rootedness and riches of any of them – and had discovered it for herself through Taizé. She now felt herself more strongly rooted in her Christian faith, developing good links with the local churches and with the Foundation. She is happy to be known as a 'new age Christian' or a mystical

Christian, something which up until then I had seen as an impossibility.

Judith had introduced Taizé singing into the community. People meet every morning in the nature sanctuary to sing and pray, and she felt it had allowed a number of community members to re-integrate their Christian faith, from which many had been alienated by their experience of an authoritarian, dogmatic and hypocritical church. The nature sanctuary had been built by one of the community members inspired by a visit he had made to Taizé. His life in the Findhorn community had enabled him to connect with the God within him. The experience of Taizé had helped him rediscover the God who is outside us. I went to the early morning Taizé singing each day, and found it very moving. On the Thursday morning, they were singing in parts a tune I thought I didn't know. They started with the bass part, then the tenor, and then the melody. As the melody came, I realised it was a tune I knew, a hauntingly beautiful one. As I thought to myself, 'I *know* this song' my eyes filled with tears and I started sobbing. I cried and cried and cried as I don't remember ever having done before. The tears just kept on flowing. I think it was the deep, deep feeling of having come home, of there being a place for me, for my faith, in that community.

Magical happenings

Then there was the Gabrielle Roth 'Five Rhythms', the most electrifying two hours I have ever experienced. The 'Five Rhythms' sound deceptively simple. They consist of free movement to five very different types and moods of music which follow a particular sequence. You are encouraged to express yourself in relation to each particular mood as the music plays. The first movement is 'flowing'; you connect with yourself, the ground and other people in flowing, circular movements. The second is 'staccato', and you define yourself and your boundaries in clear, short, sharp movements. The third is 'chaos', and you let everything go, as though you were a rag doll. The fourth is 'lyrical', and you express your lightness and beauty. The fifth is stillness, and you discover the stillness between the movements and gradually come to rest. They are easy to join in with – anyone can take part and it is up to you how much or little you move, how much or little you interact with others. People in wheelchairs can take part. You are encouraged to enter into your own space, and connect with the whole of your body as much as you can.

That evening there were about a hundred of us dancing. There was a live music group, who were responding to the mood of the dancers, with the dancers responding to the players, so that a powerful dynamic built up through the sequence. I decided that I was going to throw myself totally into the experience. By the end of the evening I felt as though I had lived a hundred lifetimes in two hours. I wrote afterwards:

I have been created, born, learnt to walk, begun to grow my body, experienced anger, aggression, dominated people, fought women, shouted at men, experienced the chaos and pointlessness of life, seduced and been seduced, made love with a woman, been more vulnerable and erotic and joyful and gentle and physical with a man than I would ever have dreamed possible, laughing in sheer joy, in a state where I was at total oneness with the music and another human being, and blessed the world. And all of that happened without any physical contact with another person and yet felt utterly real.

At the end I felt complete, very centred, strong, not exhausted as I had expected, but also in a totally 'other' world. When I came out it was as though I was walking through a different world than the one I had gone in from, a world where I didn't know anything or anyone into which I had been reborn. I experienced it as a deeply mystical experience, which gave me a feeling that I would somehow never be quite the same again.

Then there was the magic of the place and the midsummer itself. The immediate surroundings were rich in gardens and trees. Much of the building was Scandinavian in style, with lots of wood and light. A short distance away were extensive sand dunes, leading on to the sea front with views across the Moray Firth to hills in the distance. The light and warmth I experienced from the people was echoed in the light and warmth of the air. Midsummer was celebrated with a festival of dance and meditation. The choir led us into the mediation with a rendering of St Francis's prayer, 'Make me a channel of your peace'. We walked down to the bonfire which had been built on the sands. There was story-telling, drumming, some singing and talking. Peter, one of the leaders of the week and a story-teller by profession, told a moving story about the origins of the killer whale. At its climax he threw a model whale on the fire as a sign of our corporate commitment to the well-being of the planet and the whales. As he was speaking the sky lightened, and it was morning. Some stayed on to see the sun rise, while others of us went back to snatch a few hours' sleep.

The following morning I was woken by the sun early. I lay there, and my body said, 'Stay in bed' but the brightness of the sun said, 'Get up', and my body said, 'No, rest', and the sun said, 'Get up and greet the morning,' so I got up. It was a perfect morning. The birds were singing their hearts out and all of nature was glistening in the morning sun. I walked into the sanctuary garden and it was there that I had the most extraordinary experience of all. I had read about people communing with and even on occasions seeing 'nature spirits', the spirits which some say look after trees and flowers and plants, sometimes called 'devas'. I hadn't known what to make of them. As I stood in the garden a cat came up and rubbed itself against my legs. I heard a voice. I assumed it was someone calling the cat. I turned round, but there was no one there. I turned back. Then I sensed someone come into the garden. I turned round – and there was no one there, but there was a presence. It happened again. It felt as though the garden was full of spirits, moving, calling, and playing with me in a friendly way. I still don't know what to make of it, but I can't deny the reality of the experience or the sense of well-being it gave me.

Then there was the way that things just seemed to happen. I would be with someone and it was as though I knew instinctively what to say, when to touch them gently, when to be silent with them. At one point I felt it was the right moment to connect with other people. I went to the caravan opposite and a woman, Joan, was sitting outside. She was an older, married woman whom I had chatted with the previous evening, a churchgoer, trying to make sense of her experiences at Findhorn with her experience of church. We talked and I found myself sharing deeply about my life, my experience, and Celtic spirituality. Later I felt I wanted to write out a Celtic prayer and give it to her, which I did. The next day she shared that following our conversation she had had a mystical experience talking with one of the community members about York Minster, and that something had happened which meant that she was different. I could see it in her. At the end, we hugged, and I felt a healing taking place in her. Afterwards, she said she had never felt as close to another human being. I found that the more I was true to myself and what I was experiencing, the more I was connecting with other people.

There are two aspects of the life at Findhorn which take adjusting to. One is 'attunement', where before doing anything (eating a meal, having a session, doing the washing up) people hold hands, are silent together and 'attune' to God and each other and the world. It's very like saying grace or an opening prayer, but often more devotional and meaningful and focused than many graces or the sort of short prayer of the 'We'll just pray for God's blessing on our time together' type. The other is their belief in and use of 'angels'. They believe that every person, every place and every activity has its 'angel' which has that aspect's well-being at heart, and that if people attune to the angels then things will happen and be done in a more wholesome way. So there is an angel of Findhorn who guides the community, and at every session we would attune to the angel. But they also see angels as types of quality, so in the first session, we were asked to meditate and then pick up a card unseen which had an 'angel quality' on it – things like joy, peace, truth, obedience, gentleness. I had picked up the angel of truth, which strangely was exactly the same as had come my way the only time I had done anything like that before. So before each session we also attuned to our personal angel. For me, it became a very powerful symbol through the week. I decided wherever I could to live and speak out of my truth, and it was as I did so that so much seemed to happen for me, and I seemed to receive so much.

Falling in love

Then there was Ulla. The week was magical in itself. All the things that I have described were happening. And, in the process of opening myself up, being vulnerable, being the person I am as fully as I have ever experienced, and living out of my centre, I opened myself up to falling in love. It was as though God provided for that week the most perfect companion that I could have had. Ulla is a forty-nine-year-old northern European who was on the midsummer week. I had met her the first day she took a few of us across to Accounts to pay our fees, and guided us through our first meal. I discovered someone with whom I felt perfectly in tune so that we would often have the same thought or say the same thing simultaneously, someone with whom I could laugh, cry, share in depth and who I felt I could trust with anything, and someone with whom I felt a spiritual oneness which seemed to transcend our very different belief systems.

Ulla is someone I think of as being very 'new age', and we had many laughs about this relationship between (as I saw it) this wacky new ager and this Christian church worker from a fundamentalist evangelical background exploring gingerly on the edges. I have never allowed myself to fall in love in that way before and I found it a totally wonderful experience. I couldn't bear to be apart from her, and when we would meet after a few hours, I would want to hear everything she had been doing, every thought she'd had, and to share mine. And the experience was totally mutual. One morning we sat on the steps of the bungalow I was in, drinking tea, and I felt as close to her as I could ever believe possible with another person. Reflecting back on the experience, it still seems a very spiritual one. We touched, hugged, walked arm in arm, cuddled, but never mouth-kissed or acted in a way that might lead to having sex. I felt the whole of me deeply engaged in the emotion and experience, including my genitals, so it seemed as though I was touched at the core of my being, but it was as though neither of us wanted, or needed it, to lead into a sexual relationship. It wasn't, however, a question of having to restrain myself – it just somehow was never on the agenda.

Parting from her at the end of the week was the most painful experience I can remember having. On the Friday morning our group had its 'completion' session, where we shared what the week had meant to us. People were invited to share in any way they chose. Two or three chose to sing, and one man played the piano, a deep, sonorous piece of music. As he played, I found myself sobbing and was aware of many others in tears. Whenever anyone took the risk of expressing themselves creatively, I found myself crying. It was as though they were expressing beyond words something of the power, emotion and magic of the week. Then after the evening session, Ulla and I walked, and came to the point of parting. We had been meditating in the sanctuary the previous two evenings after an evening walk, often into the early hours. She said she wanted to say goodbye to me in the sanctuary. We spent some time meditating, shared something of what the other had been for us during the week, and then walked down together to where she collected her bike. We said goodbye, and I went one way, she the other. As soon as I had rounded the corner I fell on the tarmac and sobbed, with my tears washing the road. The next morning as I gradually left the place, saying goodbye to favourite places, I was crying, the tears streaming down. I felt so vulnerable. Just before I drove off I bought some things for the journey. One of the community members whom I had felt drawn to was there, and he asked if I was off, and if I thought I would come back. He said 'If you do, I shall be here,' and I started crying again. At that point I reached the head of the queue desperately trying to make out which coin was which as the tears poured down my cheeks. Fortunately, Findhorners are used to that sort of thing! For days, I carried a dull pain inside, which every so often would well up into tears. And yet strangely, in the depth of the pain, I felt alive in a different way. Three days earlier I had written in my journal, 'I feel my truth at the moment is I AM ALIVE!' In the event it proved to be something which was just for then, but which at that moment felt like a foretaste of heaven.

While all this was happening, Sirpa was travelling a very different road. I had been aware a couple of times when I had rung that things were not well with her. It was after the 'Five

Rhythms' evening that I rang her and she then shared her experience of being in the depths of despair. Over a period of months she had been receiving threatening, malicious phone-calls from an unknown 'enemy'. The stress and fear that was gradually generated put her in touch with her own untamed enemies within, and had swept her to a dark depression. She has always struggled with a very fragile trust in life stemming from horrific childhood experiences. She had been reluctant to share with me because 'she didn't want to spoil the wonderful time I was having'. I was only relieved that she felt able to talk about it, and to share. I felt deep down that it was something she had to go through. I sensed that my being away for such a long period meant that she was having to face the monsters deep inside her and, God willing, discover that they did not have ultimate power over her. Previously, I would have felt responsible and guilty about my being on a 'high' when she was down. Instead, I only felt a deep, deep love for her, and belief in the ultimate power of love and life in her.

My experience of Findhorn 'blew my mind' in the sense that it was so totally different from anything that I had expected. Instead of being in a place where I was encountering something devilish, I had arrived at a place where I felt very at home, where I found a vibrant Christian expression as part of the community, and where I found myself spiritually as well as emotionally enriched. At the same time, many of my questions and reservations are still there. I think there is a mixed message which the Community gives. On the one hand they say that the only criterion for joining is an openness to the spiritual realm and a willingness to continue growing in that within the community context. The particular belief system or religion that a person has is not important. They declare that 'We see ourselves as a meeting place for individuals with different spiritual beliefs, not as some form of new religion or cult. We believe that it is faith in God, respect for nature and goodwill towards our fellow humans that are important, not the particular form of words used to describe those ideas.'[4] On the other hand there is a feeling that adherence to one of the monotheistic religions in particular is suspect (whereas Buddhism, Hinduism and any form of mysticism is very OK), and I sense that there is more of a shared belief system among the 'inner circle' than is stated. I think it would be difficult for the community to maintain itself otherwise, and certainly for it to have grown, matured and continued to have acted as a focus for so many people in the way it has. There certainly would be major difficulties for anyone operating with a narrow understanding of Jesus as 'the way, the truth and the life', for whom the openness of community members to a variety of understandings, theologies and philosophies would be anathema. I feel the role of a place like Minton House, which stands as a bridge between the Church and the community, is critical. I felt that with a place like Minton there, and the way it seems to be enabling a softening of attitudes on both sides, I would be happy to explore membership of the community, and would certainly be happy to be an associate there. I believed that it would be a deeply enriching, growthful and deepening time, where I would find some of my Christian roots more strongly reinforced and be able to sit lightly to some of the more peripheral aspects of the Christian tradition.

Another aspect of the growing maturity of Findhorn is their increasing diversification. I have been talking about 'the community'. In fact 'the community' is not a single entity, but is made up of many parts. There is the Findhorn Foundation which is the core, spiritual group who are committed to working together and living out the fundamental principles of love. Then there are a variety of independent, self-financing enterprises which have a tighter or looser relationship with the Foundation. These include the shop, the caravan park, the ecological housing development and many others. Then there are places which were formerly part of the Foundation but are now financially independent, running their own programme, like Newbold House, a retreat centre, and the community on Erraid island, but which remain part of the community. Then there are related places like Minton House, and the two hundred or more people who live in the area and take part in its activities as associates. Very far from being a cult with a charismatic leader, it is increasingly becoming a network of associated but independent organisations, operating as satellites around a spiritual heart.

I am aware that the whole possibility of such a place being acceptable will sound alien to many Christians, for whom the very fact that a place like Findhorn talks about spirituality and angels is a sign of how dangerous it is, presenting something which approximates to the truth but ultimately is not of it. They may, as I did, have half-formed views and impressions of the community from bits and pieces of things they have heard, together with a general lumping together of anything 'new age' as being evil and Satanic, or at the very least starry-eyed, idealistic, unrealistic and misguided. All I can do is to share my experience, and encourage you, if you feel something in you connecting and drawing you, to experience for yourself, going with your critical faculties and discernment but going open to the experience. There are many ways in. For example, the community have recently produced two very honest and open publications about the Foundation and what life is like there, *The Findhorn Community* by Carol Riddell, and *The Kingdom Within* edited by Alex Walker, both published by the Findhorn Press. Newbold House is a less intense retreat centre which runs its own programme, and can be a way into contact with the Foundation. Minton House runs retreats, and is also open for people to stay for bed and breakfast. The setting is superb and the rooms are wonderful!

My sense is that the churches' response to somewhere like Findhorn is like the churches' response to the charismatic movement in its early days – something strange, Satanic, divisive, contrary to Christian tradition and to be avoided. I sense the Church has come a long way in its response to charismatic renewal, and certainly many of its choruses have found their way into the majority of mainstream churches, even if only in the 'family service'! It seems to me that Findhorn has travelled a long way in its thirty-three years, and many of the excesses of former times are behind it. Just as many house churches have matured over the years and have been become more outward looking, prepared to work alongside other Christians and playing an active role in working for peace and justice within the community as well as within individual members, so I sense that Findhorn has matured. But as with any dialogue there needs to be a mutual respect, listening and exploration. I never felt that I was being 'evangelised' in any respect, and the community would appropriately give short shrift to anyone coming to 'sort them out' or put them 'on the right path'. One of the things they have learnt painfully over the years is that the most unhelpful people are those who feel they have all the answers and, if only the Community followed their way, the Kingdom of Heaven would be just round the corner.

Of course, I may be wrong. I may have been blinded by the magic of midsummer, some might even say 'bewitched'. But I set out on the journey, trusting that God would lead me where I needed to go, and that that was the risk of faith I needed to take at this point in my life. Each of us is on our own path and needs to walk in the light that we have. Findhorn would not be right for everyone, maybe not for most, maybe only for a very few. I believe it came at the right point for me. That may or may not be true for anyone else.

Notes

1. *Selected Poems*, Kathleen Raine, Golgonooza Press, p34
2. *Journey to the East*, H Hesse, Granada Publishing 1972
3. *Flight into Freedom* E Caddy, Element 1988
4. *The Kingdom Within*, ed A Walker, Findhorn Press 1994, p34

6

In the Footsteps of the Northern Saints

I have no doubt that you have some special quality in regard to which none was found like you, and it is that quality I propose to investigate.
Monk of Farne[1]

With this great cloud of witnesses around us there-fore we must ... run with resolution the race which lies ahead of us, our eyes fixed on Jesus.
Hebrews 12:2

Journey to the North

I was relieved that I was going north up to Orkney next, far away from both Findhorn and home. I needed time to absorb what had happened to me on the island and at Findhorn, and to find some way of working through the events and deciding what to do in the light of what felt like life-changing experiences. I had chosen not to tell Sirpa on the phone about Ulla, and to talk to her at an appropriate moment, when I was clearer in my own mind about what I felt. To have time physically away from everything, off the main-land, felt a very precious gift to have at that moment. I had been attracted to Orkney by seeing a brochure when I was on

Arran, which spoke of the call of the islands and the extraordinary number of prehistoric and early Christian sites. The
fact that there was a direct bus from Inverness made it easily
accessible.

I nearly didn't make the bus. I was finding that the exploration into sacred space, and the simple fact of not having dead-
lines, meant that I was losing my sense of time, feeling that I
had plenty when I didn't. I had gone to see Pluscarden Abbey,
a restored Benedictine Monastery set in beautiful rolling,
wooded countryside about ten miles from Findhorn. It seemed
to indicate something about the spiritual energy around the
whole area that the monks were led to re-build and re-establish
the monastery during this century, not so very far from where
later on the Findhorn community was founded. I was reflecting
on this when I suddenly realised that I was in danger of missing my bus. I have never driven so fast on a single carriage-
way. Putting my own and others' lives in danger, I made the
bus with five minutes to spare feeling that the 'angel' of the
roads had been guarding me and those I overtook!

I experienced the bus ride as healing beauty. The road
hugged the coast; the sea was totally calm, shimmering blue
in the sunlight; the hills were ablaze with yellow gorse;
cormorants were fishing off solitary rocks; we passed through
little fishing villages and meadows aglow with white, yellow
and blue flowers; occasionally a single white sail could be
seen gliding over the water; every so often we plunged down
into deep rocky inlets with richly wooded ravines.

I allowed myself to feel the dull ache of pain of parting
from Ulla, to allow the occasional welling of tears to flow,
and alongside them the sheer joy of being alive. It seemed no
time before the bus arrived at John o'Groats where there was
a cool sea fog rolling in. Out of this, the ferry loomed to disgorge hordes of 'twitchers' in their green uniforms, carrying
huge tripods, cameras and microphones, looking like a BBC

outing. As we set out across the waters the sun gradually began to peer through the curtain of white, while a gentle mist remained on the water. Through it began to appear a staggering variety of sea birds, flying, diving, floating – and then suddenly we were surrounded by seals, tens of them, swimming and diving and heaving themselves out of the water to watch us. It was as though they were welcoming us to the islands, and I felt as though it was a sign that this was the right place to be, to come, at this moment in my journey.

As we approached land the mist lowered, first to a narrow band shimmering in the sunlight below the line of the cliffs, then it disappeared altogether and the next island emerged, totally clear, a lovely combination of blue and grey. A bus was waiting to meet us on the other side, and we were driven through a strangely beautiful landscape, in which I could sense the community of other islands around and had a feel of being in another world – something that I so much needed.

I had known I was coming to a different world when I rang to book a bed and breakfast for the first two nights and the landlady had said, 'Just tell the bus driver where you're staying. He'll take you on after the others get off and drop you off at my door on his way home.' Sure enough, he did, assuring me that I was 'in for a treat' with 'the best breakfast in town'. The house was a beautiful Georgian building, set in its own grounds. It was a shock to be met at the door, told by a man that his wife had overbooked me, and that I was to be taken somewhere else. I was hurtled at high speed by his daughter to a small row of modern houses miles out of town. The house was one I would never have chosen to stay in, with flowery carpets, lacy curtains and a woolly cover over the loo seat. And yet it became a temporary home. For half the money I would have been paying I was treated to a double room, superb breakfasts, and afternoon tea with copious numbers of home made cakes. The landlady was cheerful,

friendly and hospitable without being interfering. Like a
delightful child she would suddenly appear in the dining
room to say things as soon as they had popped into her head.

I felt a deep desire to communicate with Ulla and composed
hundreds of letters in my head which I didn't send, contenting
myself with a postcard. The hardest thing for me was coming
to terms with the shock to my self-image which was that of a
happily married man who was sensible enough never to fall in
love with another woman.

Exploring Orkney

I had looked forward to visiting sacred places around Orkney
on bicycle and had arranged to hire a bike on the Sunday –
the woman had assured me on the phone that she would
come and open up for me at ten. I was there in good time, but
no-one showed. The shop was called Pattersons, so I tried
Directory Enquiries. There were no Pattersons in the Kirkwall
area. I asked some local people nearby about the shop owner
and learnt that his name was Sutherland, so I went back to
directory enquiries. There were over fifty Sutherlands in
Kirkwall. I tried the tourist office, who were extremely helpful. The man remembered that it was Watty Sutherland, but
there were no W Sutherlands in the book, so he rang round
everyone he could think of to try and track down his Christian name or where he lived. Eventually he came up with his
initials, rang Directory Enquiries; exdirectory!

So I found myself with no means of transport, most local
tours having left and a glorious sunny day. I felt that God was
saying, 'Take it easy, slow down,' so I went for a walk and
found myself near a chambered tomb lying just below the
brow of a hill with views across the sea to distant islands, five
thousand years old. It had a hatch on the top of the mound
with a torch in a box, and a steel ladder down which I

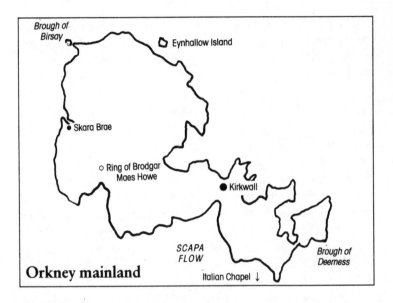

Orkney mainland

climbed and crawled into the chambers. I spent some time meditating in one of them, which I found strangely devoid of presence. In the afternoon I wandered by the sea, sitting for some time cooling my feet in a rock pool, marvelling at the variety of life it contained, and then sat in St Magnus Cathedral, a beautiful, simple, narrow, soaring building with warm sandstone somehow combining the immanent and transcendent. I rang Sirpa and felt unusually disconnected from her. I wondered if my unspoken feelings for Ulla were already affecting our relationship. As soon as my head hit the pillow I slept, the beginning of a process of catching up after the late nights of midsummer.

The following day I was at the shop as soon as it opened and finally was on a bike. I cycled round the north part of the island, some fifty miles or more. It was misty when I left but then brightened. As I came near Eynhallow (Holy Island) which can be seen across the sound, the mist lifted to reveal it to me – a remarkably similar shape to Holy Island off Arran. As I turned to cycle on, the mist came back, hiding it from sight. It felt as though I had been granted a sight of it, as though the island itself had chosen to reveal itself to me. I carried on to the Brough of Birsay, a headland which like Lindisfarne is cut off from the mainland at high tide. It has the remains of a Norse settlement and church, and I sat on the stone benches that the original worshippers would have sat on. Then I cycled on round dramatic coast scenery to Skara Brae, a five-thousand-year-old village which was covered by sand and like Pompeii has survived remarkably intact. As you wander around you can see the bed chambers with wardrobes and fireplaces, and I could picture the people going about their everyday life. Someone with a sense of humour had built a throne-like stone chair on the beach, on which I was grateful to sit and rest my legs.

I pedalled on to the Ring of Brodgar, one of the most dramatic and beautifully situated stone circles anywhere. It stands between two lakes. That day the weather was fair on one side with the lake still and sunny; on the other side the weather was stormy, the lake was covered in mist and whipped by the wind. It was as though the Ring was holding the space between the two weathers, and exuded an atmosphere of stillness. Nearby are the standing stones of Stennes and Maes Howe, which is said to be the finest chambered tomb in Western Europe. It is immense. Several of the stones used in its construction weigh thirty tons. They have tried to cut equivalent sandstone blocks today, and even using contemporary technology and tools it is virtually impossible to cut blocks of such a size. I was awed at the scale of the enterprise, and shamed that these are people we think of as being 'primitive'. The tomb was broken into by Vikings who left graffiti, some of it ribald jokes at the expense of women. It seems that little has changed! I felt more connected somehow internally by the end of the day, having felt quite flat the previous day.

That night I dreamed of being in a discussion with Bishop David about morality. David was saying, 'Think of it like a Roman road.' I questioned him, 'But do you think life is meant to be lived in straight lines?' Although he thanked me for a challenging question I felt he was clear that his role was to lay down what was right or wrong. I suspect that it reflected the internal debate that was raging in me about morality, about what I should do, about what was right.

I took things more easily on my last day on Orkney, visiting just two sites, both of which had a deep impact on me. The first was the Italian Chapel, a sacred space created out of two former army huts by Italian prisoners of war held on the island. With an extraordinary combination of skills and craftsmanship they had forged a most wonderful space out of reclaimed materials – bully beef tins, wood salvaged from ship wrecks, bits of plasterboard. I found it to be a place which not only appealed aesthetically but generated a sense of holiness and sacredness. I had expected to spend a few minutes there. Instead I spent hours, praying and meditating when I had it to myself, and wandering outside to warm myself up when coachloads of tourists came, often busily snapping and grabbing bits of information about it before dashing off. The difference when people came in who were aware of the space and its holiness was very noticeable, and I felt the power of people to respect and enhance the energy of a holy place or to suck a sense of holiness out of it. And yet the chapel receives thousands of visitors each week and manages to retain an underlying sense of sacredness.

From the first time I had looked at a map of Orkney I had been intrigued by the Brough of Deerness on the south-east of the mainland. I didn't know why. It's not on any of the main tourist routes. It is described as only having the remains of what may 'possibly' be a Celtic chapel. But somehow I felt drawn to go there. That morning however, the whole of that area lay in thick sea fog. It was cold and dank in the fog, and gloriously sunny and warm out of it. I ate some fruit shivering on the borderline, and had sadly decided that I did not want to spend the afternoon in cold, dank cloud and was about to cycle west when I noticed some rays of light through the fog. I decided to risk it, and set off into the whiteness. Within minutes I was in glorious sunshine, and the fog had completely disappeared.

The track ends near the Gloup, a dramatic natural blowhole. Although the day was still, it was a reminder of the sheer power of the sea with its ability to blast an eighty-four-metre hole through solid rock and then create an enormous cavern inland. From there it is a walk around the coast to the Brough. Its situation is dramatic from a distance. The headland looks as though it's part of the mainland. As you get nearer you see a great gulf between the two. The path plunges down the mainland cliffs to a pebbly beach which curves around forming a bay. It then ascends steeply up the headland. I needed the chain which was attached as a hand rail to the rock face to cling to in order to get up, without dizziness plunging me into a small lagoon on the other side. The top is covered in cliff vegetation. All around are circles of stones, covered by grass, the remains of early habitations. The chapel is the only standing ruin with walls about five feet high, and a simple stone bench for worshippers. The whole area is compact and small. I found myself drawn to the chapel which exuded a sense of stillness and prayer. After eating some lunch outside I was drawn back. I prayed a prayer of recommitment and trust in the God of love, and the universe of love that God has created, committing my relationships, praying for Sirpa and Ulla. It felt a deeply fitting place to be doing that; a moving location to be finishing my time on Orkney, in this place which filled me with a sense of the 'otherworld'.

A new way of being?

On the way back I followed a path which eventually dis-appeared so I ended up carrying the bike part way. When I got back on to the road I discovered that in the process I had dropped my map. It felt somehow an appropriate thing to have done, not only because I was leaving the island the following morning but because of what it signified in my life. I had a strong feeling that the map of life I have had no longer fits. I had been living my life 'in straight lines'. But I was dis-covering that life was not meant to be lived like that. It was meant to be lived in the moment, in the here and now, in the experience of being alive, loved, held, in this moment, not in a progression which starts at A and moves to B, so that one is constantly working out how far one has come, and how far there is still to go, and thinking 'When I get there then I will be able to do that'.

And I was beginning to feel that as I opened myself to life, opened myself to the God of the universe, I could trust for what I needed in that moment. As I began to open my eyes, it was as though I was seeing a totally different world. It felt as though I was a new born baby. I was in a new world, full of light and colours and wonderful shapes. And I was feeling them, exploring them, experiencing them, with no maps, no preconceptions, but open to the experience. In the process I was discovering for myself what was safe to touch, and what was dangerous. But the difference was that I could do that in utter trust – trust in the God who created me, loves, me, sustains me and is outside of me, and in the God who is inside me, part of me and leading me through an inner voice of intuition.

That had been my experience on Orkney, as I trusted where to go when things happened. Holy Island appeared; I dis-covered the Brough of Deerness. I could relax and trust the

God within as well as the God without. Whereas before I had been terrified of living in a world without a map, without clear instructions as to how to live, what to do, how to behave, how to be with people, I was discovering the excitement and above all the wonder of living in a new world where I didn't know all those things, and where every moment, every decision, every encounter was a new experience. It felt as though after thirty years of living as a 'born again Christian' I had actually been re-born into a new world, a more wonderful, exciting world than I had ever dreamed possible.

And as I reflected back on my path it seemed that my life had been relatively dull and drab in the glow of what felt at that moment like a new revelation. It seemed that doing the right things, trying hard to learn how to behave, how to talk to people, what to do and what not to do, how to fit in, had taken all my energy, so that the sense of wonder and creativity and joy in life had dulled. It was as though I had been in a living death in which I had been missing the joy of living in the moment, missing the now in my concentration on past and future. In losing my map, in the sense of no longer knowing anything, there seemed to be something deeper than anything I had known before. And that was that I wanted to continue to live, to be alive; I did not want to spend the remaining years of my life living what now felt in comparison a living death. I felt that God and love and the universe are too wonderful, too precious, not to live; that whatever else happened that was now the most important thing in the world for me. And so I found myself in the strange situation of having lost old certainties and yet feeling more sure, more certain, more rooted, more centred in truth than ever before. I felt that I could finally trust God to be God. If God is God, then I can trust that as I open myself up as totally as I know how, God will meet me and lead me. If Jesus is God then I will encounter Jesus and be met by him. But God does not need me to surround him with maps and ways of being and particular routes to encountering him. I can relax into life and allow God to be God.

Whithorn and Ninian

It was one thing to be feeling that as I came to terms with my maplessness in the brilliant sunlight of Orkney. It was another thing to retain that sense and live it in the realities of home, job, mortgage, family and institution that I would eventually be returning to. My landlady's husband gave me a lift to the bus stop for the journey back to Inverness. As I waited in the cool morning air I felt able to engage with whatever the journey would bring next. I felt a pang of grief as the bus drew into the Inverness station and had fantasies of driving back to Findhorn, finding Ulla and saying, 'I'm here, let's go off together,' but I knew that my journey was leading me on elsewhere. I was headed for Whithorn, in south-west Scotland, to follow in the footsteps of St Ninian, who historians reckon founded the first known Celtic monastic settlement in the British Isles several years before Patrick made his missionary journey to Ireland.

On the way south I broke my journey at Edinburgh, partly because there was a particular book I was keen to get hold of and I suspected that if I was to get it anywhere I would find it in Edinburgh, and partly because I remembered it as a beautiful city from all too brief previous visits. When I had had enough of the streets and shops I decided to go to the botanical gardens because the guidebook indicated that they were quite special. I discovered a place of tremendous tranquillity and beauty. I wandered gently through and came to an area with six huge redwood trees. As I neared them, I could feel energy surging out of the ground. In the midst of the trees it was almost as though there was too much energy to contain, so powerful did it feel. There were other people on benches nearby meditating. I joined them, and felt taken into another space by the powerful energies from these trees. It was almost literally an electric experience. As I came away, I had a strong sense that that was why it was important for me to come to Edinburgh, so that I could have that experience of those trees as living, dynamic organisms. Once again, an experience of sacredness had hit me unexpectedly. Now it felt as though I was being led more deeply into the experience, that I was more ready to open myself up to it.

I had high expectations of Whithorn. It seemed as though it 'would be a place where I would touch the roots of Celtic Christianity. I had come across a copy of a book called *A Way to Whithorn* about the pilgrimages made to the area, describing a way of following the pilgrims' footsteps.[2] It sounded enticing with prehistoric sites abundant in addition to early Christian ones. On Wednesday 5th July I wrote in my journal:

This is where it feels as though the blackness starts and the downside of all I've been experiencing so far. It's pouring with rain. I have been driving around the Whithorn peninsula looking for a suitable campsite and not finding one – nor anywhere accessible just to put my tent. The rain is pelting down . . . much of the peninsula is very bleak, especially on the west coast where I had hoped to camp. I have only visited one site and driven miles in the rain.

I had arrived on the Whithorn peninsula as it started to rain, my first heavy rain of the journey in that memorable summer of '95 when the sun shone almost continually and the reservoirs dried up. My journey around it felt disastrous. Every campsite I saw seemed bleak, desolate and soul-less. I stopped at St Finian's Chapel, a place of prayer for pilgrims travelling to Whithorn from the west. All I could feel was the bleakness of the place and the day and my mood. One guidebook talked of nearby standing stones. I tried to find them, failed, and got soaking wet in the process. I came back to my starting point having found nowhere that I could bear to camp. I eventually found a campsite near Glenluce, a delightful village just to the north of the peninsula, in a walled garden with a stream running through. The campsite owner kept on telling me how nice it was when it wasn't pouring with rain, and charged me a fortune to stay there. I cooked with the tailgate of the car giving some protection from the rain which dripped incessantly from the trees giving the bubbling of the stream a despondent beat.

It was a relief to wake up to a dry day and I set off in mild weather to travel some of the pilgrim way to Whithorn. Soon it was pouring again. My first call was Glenluce Abbey, a beautiful, atmospheric ruin set in a beautiful wooded valley. The warden noticed the 'Holy Island' T-shirt which I had

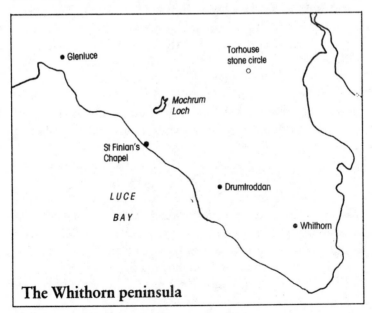

The Whithorn peninsula

bought on Arran and asked what the Buddhists were doing with the island. He said that he had friends on Arran who were concerned that the pre-Christian pagan associations of the island would be lost, and declared himself to be a *Resurgence* reader. *Resurgence* is the thinking 'new age' periodical. He also told me that the restored chapter house had wonderful acoustics, especially if I was into mongolian chants! I'm not, but I did try out the acoustics and my voice boomed back at me, sounding wonderfully sonorous, and giving me a sense of the place occupied by monks chanting the offices in devotional regularity.

I then drove up part of the pilgrim way along a lost road that wandered over the moors to Mochrum Loch. I felt a deep sense of peacefulness and stillness which seemed to come from the place, and contrasted with my general mood. I began to see how, given time, one could learn to appreciate the surroundings. The landscape is a subtle one with few outstanding features. It doesn't display its beauty immediately. As I drove on towards Whithorn I stopped to look at the Drumtroddan cup and ring stones. They lie through a muddy farm, in the middle of a field, large boulders rising out of the grass covered in strange prehistoric markings, made more mysterious by the mist. Nearby is a large standing stone. I felt the sense ·of mystery of the sacred as I stood in the damp, cool air.

As I neared Whithorn itself I felt excited. In mediaeval times it was one of the main pilgrimage places in Europe with thousands visiting, including several kings and queens. I found it curiously disappointing. It didn't speak in the way so many of the other places had. I wandered around the site trying to conjure up images of pilgrims through the ages and sense their presence, but without success. I carried to on St Ninian's Chapel, set on a headland next to an iron age fort. It was the sort of place which I could imagine making my heart leap – a ruined chapel on cliffs overlooking the sea by a small harbour with fishing boats gently rolled by the tide. My head said, 'This is a beautiful place' but my spirit was unable to feel it.

I walked around the coast to Ninian's Cave, having decided that I was at least going to do this bit of the pilgrimage on foot. I had a headache and nearly gave up as I battled with the drizzle, wind and mist and a coastline which seemed to go on for ever without revealing the cave. At last I came over a hillock and could see the beach on which it lies. I eagerly rushed forward, only to find myself on the top of what seemed like an impassable cliff. Eventually I managed to pick my way down to see the gaping hole at the far end which was the cave. Here I did feel something different. There are crosses carved into the cave which are probably eighth-century, and it seemed likely that Ninian could have retreated there for prayer. Looking out I had a strong sense of being at the edge of the world, where sea and land and sky merge into one, a place that would surely have appealed to the Celtic mind. On the way back to the campsite, I stopped at the Torhouse stone circle, a beautiful piece of marked out space. The stones are smooth, rounded and carefully graded so that each is just a little higher than its neighbour. In spite of my tiredness and general mood I felt a peacefulness about the place which gave me strength to carry on.

Cuthbert country

I was glad to leave the area the next morning. I don't think I was in a mood to do Ninian justice. I had planned to stay longer but the weather and the initial impression of bleakness of the environment had discouraged me. My spirits rose as I headed east towards Cuthbert country. Cuthbert was the much loved saint who became Prior of Lindisfarne (Holy Island) in 666. His body eventually came to rest at Durham in 995 and around his shrine the Cathedral was built. I had read about some likely sounding campsites in the guide. The first one I passed was in a beautiful location, but the caravans and tents were all crowded together and I felt I would not be in touch with nature in the way I wanted to be. The second one was worse, with the caravans and tents in orderly rows looking like a housing estate. As I carried on, I found myself driving by the river Tweed with thick woodland fringing the river. 'That's where I would like to camp' I thought, but dismissed the idea, as past experience of finding nice spots had been of surly farmers, and fenced off fields and rough, wet ground.

A little further on, however, a tiny bit of tarmac disappeared off into the wood and I decided to investigate. Round the corner it became a firm track leading down to the edge of the woods. Ahead was a field of corn sweeping down to the river. To the right a meadow swept across to where the river curved round. There was a gate through the fence and just the other side was level, dry ground. The gate was openable. I drove through and pitched camp. I was there for five nights and it felt like paradise. The river and woods were alive with wildlife – swans, ducks, terns, herons, owls. One evening I surprised a deer as it drank from the river, and watched as it bounded over the fence and danced gracefully through the corn. On only two occasions did I see anyone else when a car appeared to disgorge lovers who went for an evening walk. Twice I heard a Land Rover go past. Otherwise I was never disturbed. It felt as though I was being blessed again with a wonderful gift, and as though God was saying, 'It's right for you to continue in solitude for a time'.

My urge was to carry on visiting but I had done very little reading and knew I needed a break from travel, so I spent the first morning sitting in the sunshine by my tent reading. After a snack I set off to visit Melrose where Cuthbert became a monk. The current abbey is some way from the one Cuthbert would have known and was rebuilt in the sixteenth century.

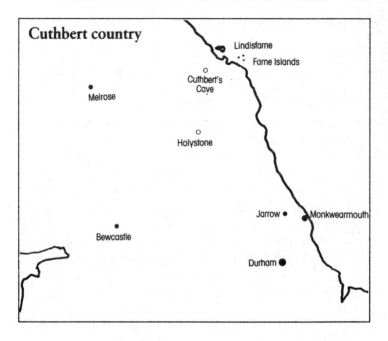

In spite of its setting in generous countryside it didn't have what I had hoped for, which was a sense of primitive Celtic church. The later building seemed oppressive. I felt more energised as I drove through the town to park by a golf course and climb Eildon Hill. It was a steep climb and I was soon sweating in the heat but was rewarded with views for miles in every direction. I spent some time trying to absorb the atmosphere of what I thought was an iron age fort, only to discover later that I was on the wrong hill! I was, however, able to picture Cuthbert on his many travels through that landscape, welcomed wherever he went because of his gentleness, concern and healing gifts, ministering the Gospel to people through his words and actions, a shining light. And I marvelled at the influence that one life totally committed to God, living out of integrity, can have.

Lindisfarne and the Farne islands

The following day I made the pilgrimage back to Lindisfarne.
I was quite nervous as I approached, afraid both that the
place wouldn't seem as special as I remembered and that it
would. The tides were perfect. It was high tide between 10.40
and 3 which meant I could arrive early and enjoy the island in
its quietness before the tourists arrived in their hordes in the
afternoon. It was a wonderful time of reconnection. For the
first time I went to the Priory as well as other favourite places.
I was very moved as I stood by the spot where Cuthbert is
believed to have been first buried. It seemed that I could feel
his presence. I went to morning communion in the parish
church. David Adam, known to several through his books of
Celtic prayers, was leading the service, a simple, low, Church
of England communion but with two or three Celtic prayers
beautifully woven in, and a short, simple, challenging sermon
on the rich young ruler. He was different to what I expected,
appearing awkward and shy in conversation but pleased
when I said how much I appreciated his books. He also said
something which has stayed with me and confirmed my own
sense. 'Some places mean you have to work to create something. We are blessed here in that this place speaks for itself
so we need to do very little.' I visited the National Trust shop
and was struck at the number of 'new age' type of books on
sale. I don't somehow associate the National Trust with the
'new age'. I bought two. The middle-aged woman who was
serving complimented me on my choice and said that someone had told her that everyone should read one of them
(called *The Celtic Shaman*[3]) before they read the Bible! It
seemed as though the 'new age' was appearing wherever I
went.

That night I had two dreams. In one I was going with one
of my colleagues from work into a tunnel – it was totally

black, very, very narrow and dark. In the other I was in a car which suddenly started going fast down a steep hill, so fast that I tumbled out. Instead of feeling frightened I was exhilarated and found I had sticky pads on my hands so I kept in touch with the ground and landed safely at the bottom. There were water sprinklers everywhere and I ran gleefully through the water. I woke feeling refreshed and exhilarated, and encouraged to continue exploring and opening myself up. I had reached a point in the book *Duncton Wood* where Tryfan, the leader of the moles, is feeling depressed and unsure which way to lead them. He remembers his spiritual director saying, 'Don't try so hard. Enjoy life,' and his companion, Mayweed, a wise mole, reminds him that when moles have a choice between two options there is always a third one, which is to do nothing. 'Mayweed has discovered that while he is quietly doing nothing moledom shifts and changes and the choices he faced shift too, so that one which seemed difficult becomes very easy . . . Mayweed suggests to Tryfan that he forgets all about the choices he has to make and concentrates instead on putting one paw in front of another enjoyably.'[4] It seemed wise advice as I was still undecided about what to do with the impact Findhorn had had on me. Possibilities of moving there and starting a whole new way of life kept coming into my mind. I read the words of the psalmist, 'Be still and know that I am God' and felt it was important not to make any decisions for now.

The following day I went out to the Farne Islands. Initially Lindisfarne was a place where Cuthbert was able to commune with God, often spending hours in prayer on a little island which is cut off from the rest of the island at high tide. But as his popularity grew and as Lindisfarne began to attract more pilgrims and visitors, he felt the need to retreat even further from society and be able to be in solitude surrounded by nature. He chose to go out to Inner Farne, a barren, inhospitable rocky island, part of a group of islands some way out to sea, but on a clear day within sight of Lindisfarne. It was only a gentle breeze when the boat set out, but in no time we were rising and falling perilously in the swell, having to be asked to sit down at times to avoid falling. I marvelled at the courage of Cuthbert who must have had to travel out in a small boat, and even more at those who persisted in making the journey out to see him. The islands today are famed for their birdlife and seals. In no time our boat was surrounded by birds of every shape and size. We were taken through a huge crowd of seals who disported themselves for our benefit, and saw the lighthouse from which Grace Darling and her father made their memorable rescue of sailors stranded on one of the islands when their ship went down.

Then we landed on Inner Farne. I was eager to encounter the spirit of Cuthbert but I found it absent, buried beneath a later chapel which was dark and made more sombre by huge dark oak pews which were shipped out from Durham Cathedral and out of proportion to the space they were in. I also found myself absorbed by the birds. We were met by terns attacking us. Wherever people walked on the marked paths between their nests the birds would hover overhead screeching obscenities and then dive and peck people's heads. Those who had been forewarned had hats. Those who didn't crouched with their hands on their heads desperately trying to ward them off. For some it was too much, and I overhead one woman call to her companion, 'Beryl, I want to go back to the boat, I don't like the birds!'

For those who braved their way through there were rich rewards in the gull chicks and the puffins – hundreds of pairs of comedians, waddling up and down, looking like a mix between a penguin with their funny walk and a toucan with their large, brightly coloured beaks. Their young are never seen. They are kept in burrows until they are old enough to fly. Then they are pushed straight out to sea where they fly off immediately, safe from the ravaging gulls. Every so often a parent would appear with fish in its beak and disappear down a burrow. At one point I could see dust flying up into the air as another enlarged its burrow, the puffin out of sight, but the fruit of its labours appearing like a puff of smoke. Further on I saw the other side of nature – a gull was devouring the corpse of a chick which must have unwisely left the safety of its burrow.

The route to Durham

On the way back to my secluded meadow I drove into what felt the middle of nowhere, in the depths of the Northumberland countryside, down a track to park by a farm and begin the trek up to Cuthbert's Cave. Cuthbert was not only a traveller in life, he travelled extensively in death, or at least his body did. Originally buried on Lindisfarne it was dug up when the Vikings invaded for fear it would be ravaged. For several years the monks travelled the country with the body, stopping where they found safety until forced to move on by further raids. They travelled north, west across to Whithorn, back east, and eventually south, finally being led to Durham where Cuthbert remains buried today. It appears that his body did not decay for hundreds of years. There is good evidence that on several occasions when the coffin was examined the body was intact, a sign perhaps of the power of his spirit and vitality. One of the places where the body was said to have rested was Cuthbert's Cave, which lies on the edge of moorland, in a copse of trees. The cave itself is impressive, huge slabs of sandstone held on thin pillars, creating a cavernous hole. As I approached, I found it both attractive and fearful. I felt drawn towards it, but also a sense of awe. Once inside, I felt a deep sense of stillness and peacefulness about the place, but the sense remained that it was not a place to be treated lightly. The names of visitors from the last century were scratched on the rocks, and a touching memorial to a husband and wife, the husband having been killed aged forty-eight in 1916, and his wife living for another fifty years after him – a poignant reminder of the realities and human cost of war.

As I approached the cave I was aware of a little wild rabbit hopping up the path ahead of me. I didn't think anything of it, until I started to leave. The rabbit reappeared on the path in front of me, and it felt as though it was leading me away. I decided to test if that was happening. I stopped, and the rabbit stopped. When I moved on, it moved on, hopping a few feet in front of me. Whenever I stopped, it stopped. Whenever I moved on, it moved on, staying just in front. It saw me on to the main path which runs out of the wood, and then it hopped into the trees and watched me as I left. Cuthbert was famed for his relationship with and care of the animal world. There are many stories of his communicating with birds and being dried by otters. I felt that the rabbit was allowing me to see something of Cuthbert's spirit, and experience it directly.

That evening I went for a walk by the river at dusk. I was suddenly aware of an owl watching me from a nearby tree. We stared at each other until he gently flew off. It felt as though I was as much being observed as observing and it struck me that there is a fundamental difference between saying, 'I saw an owl' and 'An owl revealed itself to me'. In saying the first we are detached observers of an inanimate nature. In the second we are part of a living, dynamic world which is full of fellow participants in the web of life. I imagine that the Celts would be more inclined to say, 'An owl appeared to me'.

The next day I travelled to Ladywell, near Holystone, a beautiful tiny village. Ladywell is a lovely spot, which had for me a strong sense of sacredness. The well is enclosed within a small wooded area, and rises into a large, shallow, stone pool built by the Romans. The pool still provides the villagers' water. One tradition is that the well was blessed by Ninian. It lies on what would have been a main Roman road, and it is likely that Cuthbert would have visited it. Whether either is true, it has the feel of a very special place. While I was writing this I met a lecturer from Newcastle University who told me that he had been invited to the wedding of one of his colleagues taking place there. He had dressed in a suit, and had been surprised by finding himself at a pagan ceremony, with the bride, groom, best man and several of the guests dressed as druids, and an eclectic ceremony using the four elements, symbols of which had been placed around the pool. He had felt the holiness of the place. It was also an illustration of how widespread the growth of neopaganism is becoming.

It was with great regret that I said goodbye to the meadow which had so enriched me. As I was about to pack up the groundsheet, a little frog hopped across it. I wondered if it was a symbol and reminder of transformation – the transformation I was experiencing, and the transformation that comes with being 'born anew'. I drove through dramatic Northumbrian countryside to the village of Bewcastle. Northumbria is my favourite county, hundreds of miles of beautiful, wild, unspoilt countryside with surprisingly few tourists. Bewcastle lies on the edge of moorland. It has been a site of worship for many hundreds of years. The Roman fort was built in AD 122, and it is possible that it was built over a pre-existing shrine to the native war god Cocidius. But the reason people come to Bewcastle is to see the standing cross, which rises up fourteen and a half feet in the churchyard. It is covered with the most exquisite Celtic carvings – intricate knotwork, greenery and three figures. I stood gazing at it, reflecting on the sense of the integration of human and nature as part of a wider whole. I wandered down to the river and as I did so another small frog hopped away in front of me. I wondered if someone was trying to say something to me!

I was keen to see St Paul's Jarrow, where Bede wrote his history of the Celtic church, and Monkwearmouth before they closed. I drove into Newcastle, hoping to see signs to Jarrow, but without success. Eventually I found my way there and was reassured to pick up signs to the Bede Centre. They directed me into a bit of parkland and then suddenly I found myself in a grubby carpark by a river. The only sign I could see was to the Jarrow Museum, and I knew I didn't want the museum. I then realised that the blackened, dreary looking church I had driven past must be St Paul's. I went in, and behind the church found the remains of Bede's monastery, just a few pieces of wall left. I went into the church and found myself in a place that exuded beauty. At one end is the chancel which was dedicated in AD 685 – a translation of the dedication stone is set into the wall. The chancel is beautifully simple, stone and wood. In one wall are three Saxon windows, in one of which is the oldest coloured glass in Europe. It was discovered in excavations during 1980 and dates from 681. It is stunningly beautiful, very simple like an abstract work of art. This was a place to linger, to be, to enjoy. I breathed deeply and absorbed it, feeling part of those early monks who did so much to maintain the history and culture of their time. I felt a particular sense of privilege at this connection with Bede, who hardly moved from the area and yet through talking with travellers and consulting books in the library had a lively sense of what was happening in the world around him, all carefully and lovingly recorded for our benefit.

But I was also keen to see St Peter's Church, Monkwearmouth, another early Christian centre which lies in nearby Sunderland so I travelled on, finding it without difficulty. The guides were occupied with other groups as I slipped into the church, so I made my way through to the porch which is the only original part. The doorway, porch and wall is the oldest stone building in Europe. Bede would have processed many times through it, and it is very likely that Cuthbert would have done so too. I was just in the process of absorbing the place when one of the guides came through, apologising for not having caught me before, and explaining the history. He then clearly expected me to follow him back into the church so that he could explain the rest of the church, but I was keen to continue allowing the porch to speak. Eventually, he got the message and left me on my own, but pounced as soon as I went back in to 'just tell you all about the earliest known Latin Bible which was written here.'

He was still talking as he showed me to the door. I had encountered a similar guide in another church in Alnwick who had clearly been briefed to 'talk to visitors'. At Jarrow, in contrast, the person who met me at the door was sensitive to whether people wanted to be 'talked to' or allowed to wander around on their own, while making herself available to answer any questions I wanted to ask. It struck me how important the guardians of sacred space are, especially as more and more people are visiting churches, and more churches are re-opening with volunteers keeping an eye and being available. It seems to me that there is a danger of the guardians meeting their own needs, or assuming that everyone is like them, rather than sensing who wants to be left to be quiet and who would welcome guiding around.

I had planned to have breakfast and leave for Durham after the morning rush hour. But I woke up early, to a beautiful morning. Remembering that other magical morning in Durham, I slipped out arriving in the city just after seven and finding a place to park up near the cathedral. I went in. A Eucharist was starting at 7.30 somewhere at the back. At that point I wanted to commune with Cuthbert and be in the main body, so I made my way up to Cuthbert's tomb, which is in a railed off area behind the choir. His tomb lies in the centre of a stone floor with the word 'Cuthbertus' on it. Around it are the furnishings of a simple shrine, with kneelers, and a wooden prayer pew with prayers that one can use printed out. The cathedral was totally still – not a soul moved in it. There were night lights around the tomb and I happened to have matches on me, so I lit them and spent half an hour communing with Cuthbert. I found it a deeply special time of stillness, re-commitment and of feeling part of a greater whole in the shrine set at the heart of the huge, soaring cathedral. Then I spent time sitting quietly at the back of the cathedral, before exploring the river and the woods. I came back when the treasury opened to see Cuthbert's coffin. Much of the original wood has been preserved, with line drawings of biblical characters carved into it. I gazed at it in awe, finding myself drawn back time and again to it, marvelling at being able to stand in front of the remains of the very coffin that had travelled far and wide over the country-side, carried by loyal followers, determined that it should be preserved.

My time following in Cuthbert's footsteps had been a healing time. I felt as though something of Cuthbert's presence had touched my life. In particular the experiences of the animal world had felt like ones of integration and it seemed as though I was in touch with a power of sacred places not only to move but also to heal. This sense of the special power of some places was reinforced by my next visit. I was headed for South Wales and on my way down the M6 I made a detour to visit Castlerigg stone circle set in wonder-ful lakeland scenery near Keswick. I spent some time absorb-ing the atmosphere there, feeling the energy of the place, while a woman sat with a harp which was playing itself in the wind, giving the place a haunting feel. While I was there a young man, who had driven a delivery vehicle into the car park, walked over to the circle. After a few minutes he asked me, 'Is it just me, or is there something about this place? My legs have gone all funny.' I said it might well be the energy of the place. 'The other thing I've noticed,' he said, 'is how warm the stones feel compared with the cold wind.' Some weeks later I met a woman who had grown up with Navaho native Americans and was talking about a visit to Castlerigg. I asked her if she had sensed anything special about the place. 'Oh, those stones were singing!' she exclaimed, her eyes shining.

Notes

1. *Meditation to the Most Blessed Cuthbert*, Fourteenth-century Monk of Farne. Quoted in *Fire of the North*, D Adam, SPCK 1993
2. *A Way to Whithorn*, A Patterson, St Andrew Press 1993
3. *The Celtic Shaman*, J Matthews, Element 1991
4. *Duncton Quest*, W Horwood, Arrow 1988, p688

7

In the Lands of the Celts

. . . a faith hammered out at the margins.
Ian Bradley[1]

Before you mountains and hills will break into cries of joy and all the trees in the countryside will clap their hands.
Isaiah 55:12

Places of power

I had decided to go to Wales particularly to follow up places which seemed more clearly to link pre-Christian sacred sites with Christian churches. One of the questions which sacred places face us with is whether there is something inherent in the place which different peoples and religious traditions recognise, or whether they are made sacred by being chosen arbitrarily by different societies. The presence of places with a carry over between pre-Christian and Christian times would be an indicator of something being recognised in the place itself. However, some people argue that it was simply a case of the Church deciding that if it couldn't 'beat them' then it would take them over by appearing to 'join them', so that gradually pagan allegiances became Christian ones as the Church built its special buildings on former pagan sites.

One such place is at Nevern in Pembrokeshire, just off the

165

coast road to Fishguard. The entrance to the church is lined
with huge, old yew trees, probably about sixteen hundred
years old. One of them is a 'bleeding yew'; the sap runs out
and has left dried red liquid splashed across the trunk. It has
become a focus for feminist pagans, who see it as a sign of
menstruation, and revere it as a place of the goddess. The sap
is supposed to run particularly when the moon is full. Outside
the entrance to the church there is a carved Celtic cross, and a
stone with Ogham writing on it dating from the fifth century.
In the church two more Ogham stones are built into one of
the window sills. They were found in the priest's chamber
when the church was being rebuilt. Nearby is the castle of the
local Celtic chieftain, who is said to have granted St Brynach
some land on which to found the church in the sixth century.
Among the yew trees I had a strong sense of eeriness, darkness and a feel of the power of evil, which the symbols in and
outside the church felt powerless to counter. In the castle, the
atmosphere was calmer, more peaceful. Nearby is the pilgrim's cross, a large cross carved out of a rock with some
pieces of slate added to it. I could sense energy pulsing out of
the stone; it felt to me as though there were powerful healing
and powerful destructive forces in the place.

After my previous experiences I was sceptical of using my
guide to find campsites, and more open to following my nose.
There was a sign in Nevern to a campsite. I guess I should
have been alerted by its saying 'Garden of Eden', but as the
campsite was attached to a seed nursery I just assumed it was
an idealised description of the place. I parked at the end of a
track and walked up to have a look. I came to some remote
buildings and huge greenhouses. It had a run down feel about
it. Another track led to what must be the camping field. I set
off down it, to see coming towards me an elderly man completely naked, with a woman who was clothed. What
astonished me was that neither of them appeared as though

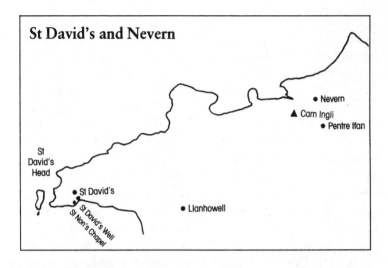

St David's and Nevern

• Nevern
▲ Carn Ingli
• Pentre Ifan

St
David's
Head

• St David's
St David's Well
St Non's Chapel

• Llanhowell

anything was out of the ordinary and they greeted me as they
passed. I carried on to find a large field, with no tents, two
caravans and superb views across to the Preseli mountains –
just the sort of place I had hoped for. I went back to the farm
and asked how much they charged. The farmer said, 'You
realise we keep this as a naturist site. Does that bother you?' I
thought at first that he meant something to do with its plant
life and asked him to repeat what he had said. When he did I
realised that it was a nudist site. It was a particularly hot day
and so it felt very natural to take all my clothes off to put up
the tent. I met one of the other people staying there on my
way to the toilet block and found that talking to someone else
who is as naked as you are is a great leveller. The communication somehow had a different quality about it than it would
have done otherwise. But I did wonder a bit why I had been
led to that particular campsite and felt that God must have a
sense of humour.

That evening I walked up Carn Ingli, the hill of the angels,
where it is said that Brynach spent time communing with

nature and the saints. In his book on Celtic spirituality in Wales
Patrick Thomas quotes a description of Brynach making wild
beasts tame at his bidding and comments, 'The Pembrokeshire
hermit emerges from the folk-memories of him as a man of
peace with both the natural and supernatural world, his
wholeness of vision apparently characteristic of the spiritual
movement of which he was part.'[2] Even on such a perfect
evening, with a light warm breeze I felt the wildness and
bleakness of the place combined with the beauty of the views
over coast and countryside. The hill is a rough, rocky outcrop, one of those frustrating places where every time you
think you've arrived at the top, you realise the next outcrop
is a little bit higher and you have to trek down and up again.
It's part of the Preseli mountains which are famed as being the
likely source for the bluestones of Stonehenge and are seen by
many as a very atmospheric place. I didn't sense the angels
there myself but I came away with a deep admiration for someone who would spend time on such an exposed and bleak spot,
and reflected that it must be fiendish in a cold wind.

I carried on to Pentre Ifan, said to be the biggest set of
burial stones in Wales. It's a beautiful and awesome place. A
huge boulder rests on three standing stones, barely touching
the tiny fingers which project from them. I marvelled not only
at how they could have got the stones up, but how they stay
in place, a wonderment shared by the four 'travellers' who
were settling down for the evening on the site with cans of
drink, but strangely to my ears talking about church wed-
dings and mothers! I felt the stones and got a strong sense of
energy coming from them, but found myself a little self-con-
scious with an audience present.

The following day I went to visit a friend who with his wife
runs a retreat and conference centre at St David's. When I was
very young we went every year to a holiday bungalow up on
a hill overlooking St David's Head, and when I was five we

moved there to live for two years, revisiting for holidays on several occasions. I have very powerful memories of the place, many of sheer joy of playing on the hill behind our dwelling, running down to the beach to play and swim, going with my pitcher to collect fresh milk from the local farm, and sitting with my mother watching the sun sink below the horizon over the sea. The fact of having no running water or electricity was no worry to me, though it was agony for my mother, with her upbringing in the upper middle class Edwardian household in New York. It was also the place I left to go to boarding school. Whenever I go back I have a powerful flood of mixed feelings, and it always feels like a mini pilgrimage.

My friend and I went to St Non's Chapel and well which are set on the cliffs not far from St David's. Round it are standing stones which look as though they once formed a complete circle. St Non was the mother of David, and the story is that she was raped by Prince Sant and where she was raped two stones rose out of the earth to mark the spot. When she was ready to give birth she found a 'special place' but the father plotted to kill the baby. As she gave birth, a great storm blew up with thunder, lightning and floods, and so mother and baby were protected from harm. An unearthly light shone around the birthplace and a spring of crystal clear water burst from the ground. The well is still used by people for healing purposes today, as it was in the Middle Ages. It is a very sacred place. We sat and talked nearby, and my friend was able to share a personal sadness and cry about it. I felt something about the place helped that to happen.

After a sandwich lunch in one of the local hotels, we went down to St David's Cathedral. Unusually, it is built right in a hollow, to avoid being seen by raiders from the sea. My friend told me that people have been known to burst into tears just on the sight of it, as it nestles in the valley. It is a very intimate, homely cathedral with a lovely warmth about it, with its simple stone walls and beautifully painted wooden roof. Behind the screen is a small area where the original pilgrim's recess lies set in what was the twelfth-century exterior wall. There is a casket in which are said to be the bones of David. St David is the patron saint of Wales who is believed to have founded a monastery on the site of the present cathedral. He had a preaching ministry throughout much of Wales and parts of England, and established a number of monasteries with a strict regime of work, prayer and simple food, including leeks from which the Welsh national food is derived. As I stood by it I had a strong sense of a prayerful presence through the centuries.

My friend then asked if I had been to Llanhowell Church, said to be sixth-century. He described it as a very special place so we drove a little inland to find it. In spite of there being several adults and children on an information hunt due to a local strawberry tea, the quality of stillness that the place generated was immediately apparent. It is very simple, much of it whitewashed. To the left of the tiny chancel is a small area where one can sit, and there is almost a tunnel leading through into the chancel. The atmosphere in that area particularly was tremendously powerful. It was a very natural place to sit and meditate, in spite of the people milling around.

After we parted I drove down to Whitesands Bay, the huge beach which curves round at the end of the coast road from St David's, and walked up to where we used to live. It was a perfect evening. I took some sandwiches with me, and sat on the spot where the bungalow had been. It has been knocked down, having been judged an eyesore by the National Trust, and the gorse is re-establishing itself. I marvelled at the beauty of the scenery as my eye swept down to the Head and then south towards Ramsey Island and out to sea. I had also forgotten that just by the parking space we used was a little cromlech or burial chamber, and I wonder if my feel for prehistoric sites stemmed from playing around that as a young child. I carried on down on to the Head, pausing in the prehistoric hut circles, and found a spot just below the top where I could sit undisturbed and contemplate the sun as it gradually sank towards the sea, bathing the whole atmosphere in a gentle light. It felt like the end of a very special day, the combination of human sharing, sacred places and perfect weather giving it a magical feel.

A holy place

The final place I visited in Wales was the most holy place of all and I nearly missed it. I was still suffering the effects of food poisoning I had picked up. I was tired. I wanted to get home. It was a detour. It didn't appear to have strong pre-Christian connections. It involved narrow, winding slow roads. But the book I was using had quoted the *Independent* newspaper commenting on how many pilgrims were now visiting it each year. And something, someone, kept me going towards it.

The road led me up a lovely valley with hills on either side to the little village named in my book as being where the church was. I found the main church in the village, parked, and walked to have a look. The church was locked which I found strange if it was such a focus of pilgrimage. It seemed recent and lacked atmosphere. Then I realised that the sign was pointing to a narrow, single-track road leading off from the village. I set out in the car. The road seemed to become narrower and narrower, as did the valley. I felt I was enwombed in the wooded hills which rose up steeply on both sides, some jagged and rough, some smooth and rounded. As I passed the odd house with no further signs to the church, I began to wonder if I had come to the right place. I had visions of the road becoming a track and petering out in a farmyard.

Yet there was nothing else for it but to keep going. And then
I came upon it, nearly at the end of the road, a sign saying
'Car Park for the church'. I walked through the gate, past one
of the largest yew trees I had seen in my travels, and entered
the church. Immediately I knew that I had come to a holy,
holy, holy place. That word kept on ringing in my ears as I
wandered around, almost in a daze. This is a special, special,
holy, holy, holy place. I had arrived at St Melangell's.

The legend of St Melangell is a simple one. In the seventh
century a prince was out hunting hares. A hare fled into a
thicket and the prince followed with his hounds, to find a
woman praying with the hare sheltering under her skirts. He
ordered his dogs to get the hare – they fled, howling. When
the huntsman raised his horn to his lips to call them back, it
stuck. The prince discovered that Melangell, a virgin, had
come there for retreat. He was so impressed that he granted
her the valley to live in, and she founded a monastery.

Parts of the present church are over eight hundred years
old. In the twelfth century a shrine was built to St Melangell
and the church became a focus for pilgrimage, but eventually
fell into disuse and the shrine was broken up and built into
bits of the wall. In the fifties an enterprising architect decided
to reconstruct the shrine, which he did in a little room
attached to the church, no mean feat as he had to work out
how all the parts fitted together. While this was happening
the remains of a twelfth-century apse were found under the
floor in the little room with a doorway which had led through
into the church. By the eighties the church was badly in need
of repair and little used. It looked as though it might have to
be closed. But through the prayer and the vision of a few, and
with the encouragement of the Bishop, it was decided instead
to restore it completely. The apse was restored and opened
up; the shrine was moved to the main body of the church. It
was only reopened in May 1992, on the feast of St Melangell,

27th May, but already has become a major focus for pilgrimage and also for healing. It has become a resource centre of prayer and counselling for those with serious or terminal illnesses, and the church has again recognised the gifts of a lay woman, Evelyn Davies, in authorising her for this ministry. It is a remarkable story of faith against the odds which has been blessed in totally unforeseen ways. And it is a holy place.

The whole area exudes a sense of specialness. The yew trees in the churchyard are estimated to be nearly two thousand years old. In other words, they could have been seedlings, and certainly their forebears were trees, when Jesus walked the earth. I spent some time in the churchyard, soaking in the atmosphere, the energy and power of the place, and the deep sense of safety and enfoldment generated by the deep, wooded valley around. I had one regret however – I had arrived a bit before the church closed. I would have loved to have remained longer. And then I heard the bell ringing. Perhaps there was a service? I hurried up to the porch, and there it said 'Compline' on Thursdays at this time. I went in. There was just the woman Reader on her own saying the service. I sat in one of the pews and joined in the parts I knew. I felt tremendously privileged to be able to join in a service which itself goes back hundreds of years, in a place where Christian worship has been offered for twelve hundred years, in such a holy, holy, precious place. It felt very fitting that I should be led there for my last visit before my pilgrimage to Ireland. After all my visits to over a hundred sites of potentially sacred space the last one was for me the most special of all. It was totally unexpected, sheer, sheer gift.

God and the earth

In following in the footsteps of some of the Celtic saints I felt I had touched many aspects of their spirituality. One was their powerful sense of place. Philip Sheldrake describes this in his book *Living Between Worlds*. 'Their sense of place was expressed in a beautiful sense of the natural world as a doorway into the sacred.'[3] Later he writes that the Christian Celts 'accepted that two worlds came together at certain familiar places in the landscape. Celtic ascetics therefore sought out places where, in some special way, heaven appeared to meet earth.'[4] He underlines that for the Celts not just any place would do. Some places were perceived as being more spiritually powerful than others. On my travels I had visited many such places and had experienced them as indeed being ones which had a special quality about them, difficult to put into words. As a result of the associations they now have for us with what we know of their link with the saints, and because many have been places that pilgrims have visited and prayed in over the years, it is difficult to separate out the relationship of nature and prayer in the sense of atmosphere they generate. But they seem to give us something that many of us lack, particularly those of us who live in cities and perhaps have moved at different times in our life. They offer us a sense of place, of rootedness and of a connection going back hundreds, possibly even thousands, of years. I was experiencing that certain places, particularly many of those associated with the Celtic saints, seemed to have in themselves a healing and energising power.

I had experienced a tiny bit of the sense of connectedness with nature and the earth which again seems to have lain at the heart of the Celtic Christian experience of God. Many writers comment on how the Celtic Christians had a very real sense of the closeness of the 'otherworld', the spiritual, transcendent world of spirits, angels, saints who had died, a world that was more real than the physical world but instead of lying far away up in the heavens was near at hand, by us all the time. It was there to be perceived by those who had eyes to see, and most important of all it was mediated through the physical, material world, so that any place could be the meeting point with the spiritual, where every tree, bush and animal spoke of God, and where, as we have seen, some places in particular had the power to focus that. In my experience of the natural world and my encounters with animals I had had a deep sense of God's presence. What was more, in my experience in the garden at Findhorn, I had sensed the very real presence of spirits and angels.

Some might think that this borders on a sort of spiritualism. The difference, for me, is that there is an element of magic in spiritualism in the belief that we can raise the spirits by certain techniques. In the Celtic Christian tradition there is a sense in which the spiritual world is not at our beck and call. If we have our eyes open to it and our senses attuned we are likely to experience it, but it will be an experience of disclosure. Being still in sacred places will increase the chances that we will experience the 'otherworld' in direct ways, but it is not a guarantee. The later Celtic prayer tradition collected from the western isles by Alexander Carmichael in the last century, the *Carmina Gadelica*, is full of prayers beseeching the protection of the saints.[5] It is not automatic and they are not within our control. It is one thing to feel the close presence of someone who has died but quite another to believe that anyone has the ability to summon them up at will.

The other fear in seeing the world as 'charged with the grandeur of God', as the poet Gerard Manley Hopkins expressed it in his poem *God's grandeur*, is that we will fall into an animism where we will be worshipping nature as a god, or as God, a view known as pantheism.[6] But throughout the Celtic Christian tradition is the deep conviction that God is the creator of all. When we encounter, are awed by, wonder at a particular element of nature, whether it be a single tree, the moon, a stupendous view, or the power of the elements in a storm, we are being encountered by the creator God who is using the medium of creation to communicate with us. The psalmist frequently calls on the elements of nature to worship God, and sees them as expressing God's glory. For them to do that they have to be animate, alive, living, expressing the qualities of delight, wonder, worship, joy. The mistake is not the experiencing of any part of nature as being worthy of adoration and wonder. The mistake is to worship that part, or even the whole, as God. A living, animate, natural world with which we can interact, communicate, and to which we can listen speaks to us of the creator God who is both apart from and more than the sum of the universe and who is also totally present and immanent through it, to be encountered at any moment in any part of it.

What was more, for the Christian Celts this God about which the whole material world speaks to us is the mysterious, threefold God, the Father, Son and Holy Spirit, a God who is monotheistic without being monolithic, a God who is vulnerable, dependent, wounded as well as awesome and gloriously transcendent, a God who protects us from the evil around in the everyday things of life, as well as the God who has conquered all evil, the God whose precious blood has been poured out for me, as well as the God whose cross has redeemed the whole of the universe. And it is this God whose Spirit we encounter in the natural world. Sheldrake puts it like this in his book *Living Between Worlds*: 'God's indwelling Spirit is not merely in human kind or even in animate objects. The Spirit dwells in all things without exception. In that sense the elements such as earth and water are powerful spiritual forces because they have within them the creative energy that is God's own.'[7] The Eastern Orthodox tradition has held on to this understanding when it speaks of God having two modes of being, the immanent and the transcendent, so that we can experience God both as being fully present in every aspect of the world around us and at the same time being apart from the world.

I experience there being a fear of nature in many Christians, a fear of abandoning ourselves in love and trust to it, a fear of allowing it to call out worship and wonderment from us, a fear that we will fall into paganism. I believe that the Celtic Christian tradition says to us, 'Do not be afraid. The more you abandon yourself to nature, to the feelings it generates in you, the more you will encounter the Trinitarian, creator God, Father/Mother, Son and Holy Spirit.' That had been my experience on the island, even at Findhorn, and in my travels in the footsteps of some of the Celtic saints. And the experience had been one of enabling me to come a little bit nearer to the heart of God, the mystery of love which lies at the heart of our universe.

However, my journey was not over yet. The pilgrimage mountain of Croagh Patrick in Ireland was calling me.

Pilgrimage mountain

Saturday 29th July

Sometime in the early hours . . .
A sense of all humanity being here in the ferry waiting room into which we were disgorged an eternity ago from the bus, life tantalising us with a ferry which was loading but which was not ours. This waiting room at Holyhead is an ugly, utilitarian building. Here are the elderly, and the babies; the large families and the single travellers; the groups of young people and restless teenagers. Here are the very tall and the very short; the large and the thin; the long haired and the short haired; the young couples anxiously forming their

relationship and the older couples comfortably settled into theirs; the ones who have arrived and are waiting for buses, and the ones like us who are waiting for a ship.

People come and go mysteriously. I desperately keep an eye on the people who travelled in the same bus, trusting that they are here for the same boat. There are no boards, no announcements. Ferry officials appear at intervals and people rush up with requests, and I wonder what they are enquiring about. The only question I can think of is: 'Why am I here, now, in the early hours, in this awful place, sitting writing when any sensible soul would be sleeping in their own bed?' I suspect they wouldn't have the answer, or even the patience to listen to the question. The place is filling up; I feel my space being invaded. There is a restlessness. Suddenly there is a rush of people moving through. I wonder why, what mysterious signal has been given? What do they know that I don't? I think I should be there, but then why should I? Why am I on this pilgrimage? Why am I in this life? Stop it, I tell myself. Be . . . experience . . . allow yourself to be. 'But *why?*' my head cries. I choose to sit rather than stand and queue. Perhaps I'll miss out on a seat on the boat, but that is then and this is now, and I hate queuing.

I had just begun to relax in this place. I'm not ready to be rushed on, herded on to the next phase. A moment ago the waiting seemed endlessly long; now it feels all too short. Shall I just sit here, watch people come and go, come and go, endlessly, like the tide, until the early hours of Tuesday morning, and catch the bus home? I feel weary of travel, weary of pilgrimage, weary of sacred spaces. I guess this is the 'graveyard hour', the time when people who are awake sink to the depths, the time torturers chose to interrogate their victims. I imagine death being like this, an endless waiting in purgatory with people coming and going but my name never being called. Life feels like that sometimes -- the call never comes; I play at feeling called, at having a vocation, but I'm kidding myself. I'm sitting in an earthly waiting room and others are called and know where to go and what it's about, and I'm left not knowing, not called, and life passing by somewhere else.

The queue never seems to shorten. More join it and stand, inching their suitcases painfully forward. What happens to those at the front? Do they drop into bottomless depths of water through those doors? Are the sheep separated from the goats? Are people being stamped with secret symbols that only the initiated understand? Then the frustration begins to set in again. It *can't* take that long to check a ticket. There *must* be a better system in this world of computers where I can surf on the 'Net' to America or China in millionths of a second but can't get from here to the door without an endless shuffling of cases. Perhaps it's a major security alert and I will find my crumpled pyjamas and squashed pants displayed for all the world to see. Eventually I sacrifice my dignity, join the queue and shuffle my way on board, being met with nothing more dramatic happening than having my ticket mutilated as the offical rips part of it off.

On board ship
And still they come. More and more, streaming past, initially hopeful of finding seats, disappearing further into the bowels of the ship and returning disconsolate. The luxurious carpets and upmarket decor can't hide the basic reality – not enough seats on the boat for this number of passengers. I feel there is a parable here, but I am too tired to work it out, and people say that there is enough food on planet earth if it was shared out equally, so I glare at the people opposite who have grabbed two seats each, one for their legs. I begin to have a sense of the temporary community of the voyage as the same faces drift back and forth. I discover a benefit of being on my own. I find a spare seat, but once I am settled in it I wonder, 'Do I

want it?' Would I not be better splayed out on the floor somewhere?' But then I don't dare to go and look – seats are like
gold and someone might snatch it if I move off it. So the
luxury of the possession keeps me a captive. One young
woman sits on a seat nearby and has just settled herself down
when the woman dozing next to her opens her eyes and says,
'Oh I'm sorry, that seat's taken. There's a man sitting there,
only he's not there at the moment.' I feel for the young
woman, and am relieved when she finds herself another seat.

Morning
Somehow I am off the ferry in a sort of sleep walk and find
myself in a bus to Dublin. 'Are you going back or are you
finished?' asks the driver. I am too tired to have the wit to say,
'Both!' I slump in my seat, desperately trying to doze. I had
discovered on the ship that the place not to be was in a seat!
The seasoned travellers had laid their sleeping bags out on the
carpets and were sound asleep. Those of us on chairs dozed
fitfully, moving every so often in a vain attempt to relieve
aching muscles. In the end, in desperation, I had spotted a bit
of carpet space between four seats and had dived down, but
it was too late. Within minutes I was rudely awakened. All
attempts to be sociable have long gone. My face muscles seem
to be on strike and I can't even raise a smile. Somehow the
fact that it's daylight seems an insult. This should be a time
for sleeping.
    I am relieved to find my companion on the bus out of
Dublin to Westport on the western coast, a day's journey, is
equally tired. She is a student. She has applied for nursing
school – 900 applicants and 80 places. She is filling in by
working in a Kentucky Fried Chicken. She finished work at
6.00 a.m., gets one night at home, and then is back to work.
We both sleep. Many parts of Ireland are wonderfully
beautiful. Much of the central section, however, is not. Flat,

featureless countryside with modern Dallas-type ranch houses which seem to be all the rage, a long way from the image of stone cottages and delightful farm houses.

Late afternoon
Eventually the bus begins to empty. Soon there are just a few of us completing the journey to Westport. I stumble out and head for somewhere to eat, finding a wonderful place which does vegetarian-type food beautifully prepared for very little. The hostel is some way out of town. As I head towards it Croagh Patrick comes into view. Even with its upper part covered in cloud it looks very big, very daunting. A moment later the rain begins to pelt down, but the air is warm and I carry on.

The hostel is all I had hoped. A cobbled courtyard with flowers in tubs, leading to an old stone building with wooden beams built in 1823. Stone stairs lead up to a stone paved conservatory looking out on to a large garden. There is a dormitory on each floor with about twelve beds and a doorway overlooking the yard, through which the sacks of corn would have been passed. There are good showers with constant hot water and I am given a sheet and duvet, all for £4.50 a night. I turn out to be the only English person there, and one of the very few with English as a first language. The others are mostly French or German. I feel a bit lonely as I lie on my bed to rest, the effect of sharing a place with so many people that I don't know. The rain stops and I go for a walk out towards the mountain. I round a corner, and suddenly, there it is – the bottom half this time shrouded in cloud, but the top clear. A prominent peak, looking very, very high, not something to be climbed lightly. I feel a sense of exhilaration at being here, ready to embark on my first 'real' pilgrimage.

Evening
That night I read about the pilgrimage. A very early tradition

states that Patrick fasted for forty days on the mountain during Lent. Later versions give his stay there a colourful flavour. The *Tripartite Life of St Patrick* written in the tenth century says, 'Now at the end of those forty days and forty nights the mountain was filled with black birds, so that he knew not heaven nor earth. He strikes his bell at them, so that the men of Ireland heard its voice and he flung it at them . . . No demon came to the land of Erin after that.'[8] One of the ironies of the accounts of Patrick's life is that on the one hand he is represented as almost single-handedly driving paganism (and snakes!) out of Ireland, but on the other he is presented as a magician, a kind of druid type of figure, the main difference being that his magic is more effective. Patrick was operating in the fifth century and there is evidence of a church on top of the mountain from the ninth century, so it appears that it was a site of pilgrimage from earliest times. With a short period of decline after the famine in the 1840s, the mountain seems to have operated continuously as a focus of pilgrimage through the centuries.

One of the strange things about the pilgrimage is its date. One might have expected the main pilgrimage to be during Lent or on St Patrick's Day (17th March) and indeed the church authorities favoured that date during the Middle Ages. But there is evidence that the last Sunday of July has been a popularly favoured day throughout and the Church has now recognised this formally by organising masses and a major sermon on the top on that day each year. Some have noted that 1st August was celebrated in Ireland in pre-Christian times as the feast of Samhain, celebrating the harvest. It is possible therefore that there was an older tradition of ascent of the mountain, on the top of which a fire would probably have been lit, and that the Christian tradition has taken over an earlier pagan custom, but we can never have definite evidence of this.

Sunday July 30th

Early morning
The great day dawns. Pilgrimage day. I wake at 6.30 and join
the other 'early birds' eating a quiet breakfast. The day is
totally calm, windless, mild, dry, cloudy. The reflections in
the still water of the bay are perfect. I walk the five miles out
to the mountain. The road hugs the bay, occasionally skirting
inland, but then reconnecting with the waterside. The bay is
dotted with hundreds of tiny islands, some with cattle grazing
peacefully on them, each reflected in the water. The mountain
looms up ahead of me as I walk, its bottom half clear, its top
shrouded in mist and mystery. I am the only person walking.
Occasionally little flurries of cars sweep past, many full but at
times the road is quiet. I begin to wonder if I am on the right
day, in the right place. Is a major pilgrimage happening?
There are no signs anywhere. I am reassured when a car stops
and they ask for directions to Croagh Patrick. 'Just keep
going,' I say confidently. A car stops going the other way. Can
I direct them to Westport? I do so, equally confidently, and
begin to feel like a native.

As I get nearer, the huger the mountain appears. I wonder
what am I doing there. Am I mad to be attempting this? Why
not just go back? Or at least hitch a lift to get there? Why subject my body to what appears to be an agonising climb?
Something keeps me going, and I arrive at the little village of
Murrisk and the parked cars begin – every available inch of
kerbside, every field, every patch of grass has been turned into
a car park that stretches as far as the eye can see. I count seven
hundred cars along the bit of road I walk on. Then I come to
the first stall of pilgrim's sticks – sturdy poles of varying
thicknesses and lengths. I choose one and gladly pay a pound,
feeling that now I am a proper pilgrim, complete with my
staff. Little do I realise how important that stick is to become,

keeping me from falling, and providing the support I discover I desperately need to get me up and then down the monster of a mountain.

There are a few more people here. I round a corner, and suddenly there it is – the path leading up the mountain. I stare in wonderment. The path is thick with people, looking like ants crawling up and down, a seething mass of humanity disappearing up into the mist. It's not even nine o'clock on a Sunday morning and people are already coming off the peak. I can see their tiredness in the eyes and their bodies. They are hobbling stiffly, often falling, some supporting each other over the last stretches down. This is no picnic, in spite of the many families who are setting out. The atmosphere is a strange one – serious, determined, yet relaxed. In the men's loo at the bottom I hear one man calling, 'This'll sort the men out from the boys.' My hesitations and fears begin to be replaced by a determination. I'm here, and I'm going to go for this, and I've come all this way to do it, and I will not be defeated by it. If they can do it, I can and I will.

There are a few stalls at the beginning of the path selling religious bric-a-brac, others selling drinks and snacks. Then the statue of St Patrick which stands near the bottom, and a plaque reminding people that this is a holy mountain, and informing them of the full pilgrimage which if done in the months of May, June, July and August, will gain them a plenary indulgence. My protestant hackles quiver a little at this, but I am determined to do it. I can manage the walking around the various points, I can say the 'Our Fathers', stumble my way through most of a 'Hail Mary' and say as much of the Creed as I can remember. I am stumped, however, at the need to 'pray for the Pope's intentions' at the chapel at the top. What on earth, I wonder, are the Pope's intentions? How would I know? How would I pray for them if I did know? And given that many of my views differ radically from the present Pope's, could I in all conscience pray for his intentions anyway? I decide to leave this bit for those in the know, and do as much of the rest as I can. As I strike upwards on to the moors npast the bubbling stream which merrily dances its way down, I am met by the Protestant protestors, many of them grim faced, one smiling as she hands out leaflets, most of which get thrown and trampled into the mud. A little higher up an evangelistic group are singing choruses. 'That's all we need,' quips one of pilgrims, '*Sisteract* meets *The Sound of Music*.'

Mid-morning
Soon the stream is left behind, and the real, hard, upward slog begins. Conversation disappears. Everyone is concentrating on putting one foot in front of the other, keeping their foothold, avoiding bumping into the sweaty, glowing, stumbling, exhausted people who are coming down, trying not to think too much of the coming agony and just concentrating on the next step. The impetus is up. The people behind, the people in front, are all impelling me up. And the fact that the people coming down have got there, have been to the top, have been initiated, have *survived* the ordeal is a spur to keep going. Every so often I pause to catch breath and take in the expanding view of the bay dotted with its islands, and marvel at the continuous flow of people up and down, and then I am impelled upwards again.

I am surprised by the people who form the band of pilgrims. I had assumed that a devotional pilgrimage would attract the typical church congregation I am used to, predominantly women, predominantly fifty-plus. I counted twice as many men as women. Men of all ages; the older men noticeable in their suits and ties and peaked caps, but men of all ages. Then the second biggest group was young people between sixteen and twenty, again more young men than young women but infinitely more young people than I am used to seeing at religious events. Then there were the families with children of all ages, keeping one another going. I talked with one older man who was doing the pilgrimage for the thirty-eighth time. This one was 'to ask a favour from God'. He was going at it with a quiet, impressive, determined gusto.

As I got higher I had to concentrate more as the slope became steeper and steeper, in places wet and slippery, in others perilous, and as the numbers of people coming down became more numerous and I was trying to avoid bumping into them, or stepping on those going more slowly upwards, or being in the way of those climbing more quickly. At one point there were shouts of 'Make way, please, make way' and we crammed to one side as a stretcher with an older woman on it was carried past. (The talk in the pub that evening was that she had died.) The effect was sobering and people climbed on in deeper silence. And then I was at the shoulder, the point of respite, where the path levels out for a few yards, and it was still possible to discern bits of land below as the mist rolled back and forwards. Above, all was grey white murkiness of mist with people disappearing up into it, and appearing out of it. Here the pilgrimage proper seemed to begin. We were at 'Leach Benain' the first station. Pilgrims walk around a large cairn of stones, seven times, saying seven 'Our Fathers' seven 'Hail Mary's' and a creed. Most were walking in silence. People silently joined in the circle and then peeled off upwards when they had done their seven rounds. I found the atmosphere deeply moving; suddenly I felt I was in another space, a space which was about something outside of myself. This was no longer any climb; it had become a religious, sacred experience.

Midday

It was here that I made my decision. The traditional way of

doing the pilgrimage is barefoot. I had not been aware of any others in bare feet, but there were two without shoes going round the stones. I had been prepared to do it barefoot. I decided to go for it. Thinking that I could just go round the stones barefoot and then put my shoes back on, or if necessary could put them back on at any point, I sat down and took them off. Initially the ground felt cold and hard, but soon it felt friendly, comforting, supportive. I joined the others encircling the rocks, and felt myself entering a different rhythm. Then I peeled off on to the sheer, agonising hell of the second half, the ascent up what felt like virtually vertical scree, which every so often would slide from under my feet, pushing me back down, forcing me to inch my painful way over the same stones again. To begin with, going barefoot was a novelty and I revelled in it. I enjoyed the way I had to be mindful of every step. I enjoyed the skill I began to develop of being able to sense when a stone would or would not hold me, and which stones were smooth enough not to be agonising to step on. As the slope went on and on, however, the novelty began to wear off. I was aware of soreness every time I put my foot down. There was no respite. The only way was up. The only way up was by walking. And walking meant one sore footstep in front of another. Now my stick was no longer a luxury; frequently it was the only thing keeping me upright; frequently too it was all that prevented me from sliding back down again. It seemed as though the agony was set to last for ever, so it was a shock when I heard someone say, 'You're nearly there', and a moment later I saw the rough tents with cans of drink for sale, with the donkeys who had hauled it up there standing patiently by, and realised that I was actually there, on the top. In the thick mist, the only other clues were the levelling of the ground and the crowds of people.

I knelt, gratefully, and said my prayers. Then I could make out the chapel in the distance so I joined the crowds who were

listening to a sermon from the Archbishop of Tuam. I sensed
a sensitive man, a gracious man, in tune with what it meant
to people to be there, in tune with the combination of a celebration of nature and faith, gently encouraging the lapsed back
into a living faith. Others were making their way round the
chapel, doing their fifteen circuits. I joined them, blessing the
odd bits of smooth concrete, to relieve the agony of the tiny
stones on the rough ground. I broke off my circuit to listen to
the words of consecration, and then joined hundreds of
others as we fought our way in to the narrow passageway
where the wafers were being distributed. I headed for the one
woman administrator and was pleased to see many others
doing the same.

I had been vaguely aware of television cameras being there
but I was totally unprepared for what then happened. As I
finished my last circuit a man sidled up in a friendly way.
'Have you finished your three times round?' he said. 'Fifteen,'
I corrected him, 'yes.' 'Would you mind answering one or two
questions about why you're here?' That seemed reasonable.
The next thing I knew I was being pushed round the corner,
made to look as though I was doing a circuit while a cameraman walked backwards in front of me with his monstrous
instrument glaring at me. I had just started my answer to the
first question when the cameraman disappeared backwards
over a stone. 'We'll have to do it again, but we're running out
of tape, so go straight into the answer'. Feeling foolish, I bur-
bled something. Then it was a 'thank you', they all disappeared into the mist, and I was left feeling a strange sense of
let-down and thinking of all the things I wished I had said. I
wandered around feeling a bit lost and alone. Then I gradually re-connected with why I was there, what this was all
about. I became aware that in the milling of the people on the
top I had very little sense of place, and the sense of devotion
was dissipated by the different agendas – those just there for

the climb and picnic at the top; those joining in the continuous masses and those doing the rounds of the chapel, trying to make their way through the two other crowds. And still the people came, pouring up.

Early afternoon
I wander around the top. People notice that I am barefoot. They are curious. 'How does it feel? Have you trained your feet for it? You are brave.' Some say they have thought about doing it but never dared. Others say they would never consider it themselves, but it is clear that they are glad that some of us do. I discover a comradeship with the few other barefoot pilgrims. It is as though we share a depth of experience which the others have no access to. It is somehow a sense of being as fully in the pilgrimage as we can get, and a strange sense of humility, of privilege, rather than bravado about it.

I decided to take the plunge back down again, and discovered painfully the truth that every mountaineer knows. The easy part is the way up. There is the call of the summit, the goal to aim at, the sense of purpose, the sense of the unknown, calling one upwards, higher and higher. Getting down is about survival, about continuing to exist. It's going back over old ground. It's about going back into whatever one has climbed out of. And to cap it all, it is physically harder. Every step becomes pure agony. The way down seems endless. The only reliefs are the little conversations with people resting on their way up, seeking the odd word of encouragement to give them, knowing that the fact that one has been at the top is in itself an inspiration, helping them to believe that they can do it too. And especially if you can do it barefoot, then they in their shoes will surely make it. The stones seem to go on for ever.

And then I am back at the first station, out of the mist, and sitting in the sunshine, watching the encircling of the stones

and the powerful effect of it, even on those who push on up.
And then the most difficult decision of all. Here I took my
shoes off. I could put them back on with honour. I could tell
myself that that part is the real pilgrimage. And yet it would
feel incomplete. So I decide to persevere with no shoes. On
the scree the stones are large, sometimes smooth, sometimes
sharp in places, but it is usually possible to get a foothold.
Going on down, the stones are tiny, sharp, unavoidable, pin-
pricks of agonising pain at every step. Others hurry past in
their shoes, stumbling, slipping but making progress. I hobble
along, using the stick to bear my weight as much as possible,
seeking out the odd places where warm, silky mud oozes and
bathes my feet with gentleness before the next painful pin-
pricks of sharp stones, more agonising in contrast to the
soothing mud. One woman comments 'Now, that really does
look like penance.' 'It certainly feels like it,' I gasp. I no longer
wonder why I am doing it. I am doing it because I have to do
it, because for me at this moment there is no other way,
because this is a way in which I can enter into the heart of pilgrimage, which is about meeting whatever comes, not finding
easy ways out. The cars at the bottom of the hill never seem
to get any bigger. The houses remain obstinately small. There
is no opportunity to look at the view because each step is
perilous, each could send me tumbling, and there are the
people pushing their way upwards, unaware that they have
the easy part . . . until . . . until . . . the bottom seems nearer
. . . is nearer . . . there is heather . . . the stream reappears . . .
there is grass . . . the statue at the bottom . . . the Archbishop
greeting people, asking me about my feet, handshakes with
the clergy by him . . . and then the most wonderful, glorious
moment of plunging my aching feet into the cold waters of
the stream. I've done it! The sense of achievement is immense.

To my surprise the five-mile walk back to Westport feels
easy. I am uplifted; I have energy. The shoes feel strange to

begin with, but I bless the fact that I am not having to walk barefoot on the little stones. I catch up with an American who comes to Ireland on holiday every year and 'always does Croagh Patrick' when he comes. For him it is important to walk out from Westport – it is part of his pilgrimage. And so we walk in comfortable silence, until I peel off to the hostel and one of the most delicious cups of tea I can remember.

Evening
It would have felt wrong to have simply gone to bed, so I ate in one pub, with my back against the wall of the little garden overlooking the bay enjoying the sunshine, and then went to the pub which everyone said was the place for 'the real thing' – Malloys. I make my way to a little room at the back, and sit, feeling alone and lonely as everyone else seems to know each other or to have made friends. Then someone sits next to me, and chats. I ask him what he does. 'Oh, I travel around the world singing and story-telling,' he says casually. I later discover that he is a local celebrity with an extraordinary voice, and the ability to start a story in a room full of loud conversation with such authority that everyone quietens to listen. He moves on to chat to other customers. A man my age takes his place. I chat and discover someone with whom I can share in depth. He had been up the 'reek', as the mountain is known, the previous day. Although not a practising Catholic he says the first time he had done the pilgrimage he had burst into tears at the top because he was so moved. He, however, chooses to do it when there are fewer people, and I realise that although I had gained something in doing it 'on the day' I had also lost something in the sense of the place itself and its power. One day I shall go back not on the last Sunday in July.

Then the musicians arrive and sit at one of the tables. Within seconds the place is transformed as they start to play. Eyes are glowing, feet tapping. Couples who have been lost for words with one another close together and become unitedly caught up in the music. I am squashed up against my new companion, with a very attractive woman nestling against me on my other side. The playing is fast, furious, lyrical, soulful, soft, by turn and always brilliant. Other instruments appear and join in. Talents are discovered. Every so often there is a cry of 'Hush, hush, this man from Sligo is a singer,' and we are transformed into another world as someone sings soulful ballads of the heroes of his area. Then it is a woman singing a deep sonorous jazz melody. Each time a new singer is discovered the musicians listen intently, pick up the rhythm and melody, and play an accompaniment, but always careful not to dominate the singer. The 'celebrity' sings and tells stories. People replenish their glasses rapidly. I am content to nurse a glass of wine and soak in the atmosphere, transported into another world where time has no meaning. It is a shock when the landlord calls time, and we stagger out into the cooler air of the early hours.

Monday 31st July

Morning
I was out the moment my head hit the pillow and I didn't surface until after ten in the morning, my body taking the rest it needed. My limbs feel sore but not too stiff; my feet are a little sore but not painful, and not damaged. I feel a bit sick however – too much sun, too much exercise, a bit groggy. The bus is full on the way back, everyone jealously guarding their space, hoping for a companion who isn't too large, or doesn't smell, or talk incessantly. I have one for a short time who talks continuously. I deliberately keep quiet, marvelling at his ability to keep on thinking of things to say. Gradually as the journey progresses and there are fewer changes the bus becomes a community. We have a major stop, and afterwards

there is an atmosphere of energy and aliveness. Later on, as
though on cue, the atmosphere changes and all the children
are crying, and parents are quarrelling and there is a general
edginess. Then a sleepiness takes over and the community is
quiet. As the end of the journey begins to become apparent,
the mood changes again – all over the bus people are making
friends with the children who before had been only seen as a
nuisance.

Evening

There are the final indignities of travel. The arrival at Dublin
bus station to be told that this is the bus you need to get on,
but you can't get on it until you've gone to that window there,
queued, showed the man your ticket, got another ticket, come
back here and shown it to me. The man in the window didn't
even look at my ticket, just asked me where I was going. At
the ferry, instead of walking the few yards from the waiting
room to the ship they took us in a bus. It was swelteringly
hot, airless, and we sat for what felt like hours in a queue of
cars, coaches and lorries to get on to the ship. We then had to
climb numerous flights of steep stairs to get to the deck. It was
too much for many. 'I'm never going to travel with this company again,' people muttered as they made their way up. I
had my stick with me. People were curious but as soon as I
mentioned the pilgrimage they understood, and confessed
that they had always wanted to do it but had never quite
made it yet – maybe next year.

    This time I knew what to do on board ship. I headed for the
carpet, marked out my space and zonked down. It was a long
time before I got to sleep. The next thing I knew was a distant
voice: 'All foot passengers to deck number three, all foot passengers to deck number three.' Groggily, I collect my things,
joining the hundreds of half-asleep passengers wandering
around trying to find deck number three. We find what might

be it, but that is a car deck, so we go back up, then back down, then on to the car deck where we are herded on to buses. Many have to stand. We wait and wait and wait and wait while lorries rev their engines and the bus fills with fumes until eventually we are ejected. We stumble into the waiting room, through the waiting room and out of the waiting room. An official stands at the door. 'Where are you going?' he says. 'Liverpool,' I say. 'Sharkeys or Bus Eireann?' It's three o'clock in the morning, I am still half in deep sleep and I know that neither of those is right. I stare at him gormlessly. How can I say one or the other when I know neither are right, but I can't remember what ticket I have. And if I say, 'Neither' I am afraid of being sent back. I ask him to repeat the choice, but it doesn't help. 'Show me your ticket,' he says brusquely. I am about to scrabble in my bag for it when inspiration strikes. 'Eurolines,' I say. The magic works. 'Third bus along.' I arrive at the bus. Another official. 'Manchester?' he says. I groan inwardly. 'No, Liverpool.' 'Bags in the next compartment.' I sink thankfully on to a seat and doze fitfully. There is a taxi at the bus station; Sirpa has remembered not to bolt the front door. I am home! My travelling is done. But how can I re-connect? What sense can I make of the journey?

Notes

1. *The Celtic Way*, I Bradley, DLT 1993
2. *A Candle in the Darkness – Celtic Spirituality in Wales*, P Thomas, Gomer 1993, p64
3. *Living Between Worlds – place and journey in Celtic Spirituality*, P Sheldrake, DLT 1995, p4
4. ibid, p5
5. *Carmina Gadelica*, A Carmichael, Floris Books 1992
6. *Poems and Prose of Gerard Manley Hopkins*, sel W H

Gardner, Penguin 1983, p27

7. *Living Between Worlds – place and journey in Celtic Spirituality*, P Sheldrake, DLT 1995, p82

8. Quoted in *Croagh Patrick: An Ancient Mountain Pilgrimage*, H Hughes, No publisher, p14

PART 3

Return and Reflections

Down to Earth

This journey is not to the sacred place, but it is a journey to find and befriend the sacred centre within, the place which is everywhere and nowhere, centre and circumference, which in Christian tradition is known as the soul.
B and T Butler[1]

They are strangers in the world, as I am.
John 17:16

Re-connecting with home

I was very happy to see Sirpa again. She was eager to show me all the changes she had made in the house, exercising her remarkable gift for interior design; I needed time to re-connect with the space before I rushed around looking. Gradually we settled down and I talked about bits of the experience. As I was kneeling down picking something up by the downstairs loo door, she asked: 'Did you have sex with anyone?' I said, 'No, but I did get very close to Ulla.' She said, 'I knew from the way you mentioned her. You've fallen in love, haven't you?' I said, 'Yes.' Then gradually she asked more and I talked about Ulla, about Findhorn, about feeling that it could be a place for us as a family to be at, to grow spiritually in, to find a way forward for our life. She was still feeling her depression and said, 'A place for you; not for me. I feel there is no "place" for me. If you choose to go you will need to go there on your own. Perhaps that is something you need to do for a year.' Immediately my fantasy began to run wild. After all, if I was going to leave my job this was the time to do it, with a positive report of my work having been made, a new direction having been given and therefore an ideal time for a new person to come in and build on the foundations I had laid.

But then the realities earthed both of us – the mortgage, the effect on family life. But what felt important was that we together were talking about it, opening ourselves up, both willing to look at different possibilities. Much of our conversation took place in our sauna, which is one of the many joys of the Finnish culture. Far from being a luxury there they are more common than bathrooms and are a focus for communal life. They provide an area which in itself seems to be a sacred space that feels very safe, where risky things can be said and held. At the same time, I was aware of how easily Sirpa can be generous and deny the deep hurt inside. It felt that we were re-connecting well and there was an ease and openness in our communication which seemed to lead naturally into some wonderful love making. I was beginning to discover that this new world I was in was full of surprises.

Two days later I went to see Sister June, to share my journey up to that point. It was wonderful to share with someone who understood so well all that I had experienced, but who was beautifully straightforward. 'There's no question of your moving to Findhorn,' she said. 'You've got a mortgage and commitments here.' And I had a deep sense that if it was right for me, or as I believed would be the case, us, to move to Findhorn then the blocks in the way would disappear and circumstances would work themselves to make it possible. I would not have to push against circumstances and reality.

Reality would mould itself, if that was right. That also seemed to be part of this new world, where things seemed to happen naturally. I also found that as I talked with June I reconnected with the experience; both how important the contact with nature had been, and how I needed to let go of everything *including* God in order to discover God.

That left though the question of my relationship with Ulla. The longing, desire for connection was still there and very strong. I could not deny that. Whenever I thought of her, I found myself in touch with a very deep, vulnerable, beautiful place inside me. And yet deep down I felt that to see her again at this time would be unhelpful and confusing to both of us. I decided therefore that I wanted to communicate with her by writing to her and longed to hear from her, but that I could not offer her anything more. I wrote to her to that effect, leaving it open to her whether she responded or not. She replied in a letter which I found very moving, confirming her sense that I should stay where I am at the moment. We have continued to correspond occasionally.

As the summer developed it transpired that while I was following a particular route which seemed at times to take me in a different direction, Sirpa was on a parallel but very different journey of her own. While mine seemed to be leading me to the heights, hers at times was plunging her into the depths. At the same time she was discovering new directions for herself and also experiencing magical elements. She was finding that when I was away people seemed to gravitate to her and come into her life. She has a gift for creating space which people often describe as 'sacred'. Having transformed the large old Victorian house where we live, she has turned her attention to our garden which has suddenly become a special place, beautifully enhanced by a rough, wattle summer house which we put up in an inspired morning and which draws people to meditate in it.

One weekend while I was on my travels she decided to organise a brunch. It was a glorious, sunny morning and a number of people came. She had made a garland of flowers for herself, and suggested that others did the same. People have told me with glowing eyes of how magical that time felt. Sirpa took some photos and just looking at them I could sense the joy, the deep relaxedness of people, and their delight. Afterwards one of the participants said that they felt there was something very sacred about our garden now. Another piece of magic was a shared one. It was nearly midnight on a beautiful warm summer's evening. Sirpa wanted to drink lager in the garden. I suddenly remembered that it was nearly my birthday and I would be away for it. We decided to celebrate. We lit candles in the meditation hut, and took out a bottle of sparkling wine, and a bowl of summer fruits with dark brown sugar and cream. Sirpa produced my presents, and we sat together in the candlelight in a delicious intimacy. Even the hateful snails joined in, serenading us with a gentle crackling.

To our delight it felt as though the two very different journeys were bringing us back to a similar point. As Sister June suggested when I shared with her, it is as though we needed to each separate from the other in order to discover more of our own identity. From that we can come together in an even more mature relatedness. But in order to discover that we, I, had to take the risk of setting out on my own, open to whatever came my way.

Falling in love again

It seemed as though things were settling down and sorting themselves out. I was pleased at the decisions I was making, painful though they felt. I believed that I was handling the experience of having fallen in love with maturity, and relieved that I was rediscovering how much I enjoyed my relationship with Sirpa. That, however, was until I met Jan. The relationship with Ulla had grown over a few days. The relationship with Jan was instantaneous, love at first eye contact, a frighteningly wonderful piece of magic woven at that holy, holy, place in Wales, Pennant Melangell. I had gone there a few weeks after returning to work for a one-day conference on Celtic Spirituality. The place felt as special as I remembered it as we sat in the church listening to Donald Allchin drawing out its significance. We went over to Evelyn Davies's garden to eat the packed lunches we had brought. I sat down and chatted to the man on one side. Then I turned and started talking to the woman on the other side. It turned out that she lives not far from where my brother has moved to in South Wales, and the previous day had happened to visit his neighbour and heard about these people who had recently moved in. As we spoke we discovered a harmony, a closeness which was utterly surprising and felt totally absorbing. We were asked if we would come to the church and be interviewed for local radio. The interviewer never got to us, but we didn't mind. We were locked into the delight of discovery, of sharing in which time seemed to stand still.

Jan brought out a tiny, multi-coloured stone she had found on Iona and had carried with her ever since. On an impulse she said, 'I would like you to have it.' Contrary to my usual instinct to say, 'Oh no, I couldn't' or 'Are you sure?' I had no hesitation. It was right to accept it, to treasure it. I have it still on my desk at home. I had to leave early so I had decided to miss the communion service and walk for a few minutes up the valley. Jan asked if I wanted to be on my own or if I would like company. We walked, sometimes in deep, companionable silence, sometimes exchanging information about ourselves, sometimes sharing intimate feelings. We sat on a bridge overlooking a stream, allowing the sound of the rushing water to

flow over us, and gazing into each other's eyes. It was a
wrench to tear myself away. My longing was to stay with her,
to go somewhere to eat, to continue enjoying a depth of intimacy and a feeling of freedom in each other's company.

That night I wrote to her, a long, passionate letter, expressing how much the meeting had meant to me. Our letters
crossed in the post. It was as though a well-spring of passion
had been unleashed. We wrote letter after letter to each other,
pouring out our feelings, hopes, desires, experiences. I scanned
the post eagerly each morning. The passion released spilled
over into other areas. I wrote other letters to people, discovering an energy and pouring my feelings on to paper. There
was such an attunement between us, such understanding,
such harmony, such one-ness, every word full of significance.
It felt as though I was caught up in something over which I
had no control, over which I wanted no control because the
experience was so ecstatic.

And yet I was shocked – shocked at how it had happened,
how I could have made myself so open that it happened. It was
one thing to fall in love once on a sabbatical journey. It was
quite another to come back and then fall in love even more
passionately with someone else. I rationalised it – this is not a
young sexy woman that I have fallen in love with, but a mature
professional woman with grown-up children – but that did not
alleviate the shock to my self-image. Nor did it do anything to
relieve the strain on my relationship with Sirpa, deeply hurt by
the passion that I was pouring out to another woman, smiling
bravely as she handed me 'Another of your love letters' but
feeling the pain of rejection. Eventually, I knew I had to act.
Either I had to see Jan again and see what that relationship was
about, how much reality it had, how much fantasy, or I had to
end the passionate letter-writing. Wise friends advised me that
there could be no future in a relationship with Jan. I was at a
crossroads and had to decide.

I decided to rediscover my feeling for Sirpa. I wrote her a love letter and found it pouring out – all the things I love in her, about her, all that I enjoy. I wrote to Jan saying that I felt we should stop writing, that if it is right for us to meet up some day then that will happen, but that her sharing had deeply enriched my life and would stay with me and we did not need to know why we had met and shared so intensively, but only to enjoy its fruits. It was an intensely painful letter to write. A huge hole seemed to appear in my life with no more letters from Jan. The strain in my relationship with Sirpa has taken time to heal. I felt pain through much of the winter with only tiny stirrings of passion for everyday life re-awakening, which seemed as fragile as the tiny buds covered with snow. What seemed like a clear decision was followed by months of inner turbulence which I gradually realised was as much about a tussle between two sides of myself as it was about the two women. The resolution came over Easter when I met Jan again and discovered that the person I had built into a fantasy of freedom and creativity in my mind was someone wonderfully ordinary with whom I feel a natural affinity and friendship but no more than that. Meeting her again has released me to rediscover my true depth of passion for Sirpa, an experience which has strangely enriched and matured our relationship leading to a re-commitment to continuing to share our life together on our twentieth wedding anniversary witnessed by friends.

Re-connecting with the Church

An area which had bothered me was how I would re-connect with the Church, the institution that employs me and yet whose apparent inability to meet so much of my longing for God had catapulted me into this journey of exploration. My first encounter was an invitation to the ordination of a friend in Liverpool Cathedral. How would I experience a service which lies at the heart of the Church's' institutionalisation, the clericalisation of its leaders? I fully expected that to be the moment when I decided that the institutional church and I would have to part ways, mortgage or no mortgage. Instead, I found myself at a moving, and spirit-filled occasion. There was a deep sense of devotion and spirituality. And I found that the words which formerly would have stuck in my throat all made sense, but in a new way. It was as though I was hearing things differently, at another level. It was a setting where, to my surprise, I found myself very happy and felt a tremendous sense of God. This new world was turning out to be a strange one indeed, where all the maps had disappeared and where even the things I expected to bite could turn out to be embracing.

I felt I wanted to re-connect on a personal level with one of my colleagues. We arranged to spend an afternoon together and went to Formby sands, where we took our shoes off, walked in the sand and the sea, talked and hugged. When I got into the car, she said directly, 'Talk. Tell me about it.' To begin with I was tongue-tied, not knowing where to start, but then it all poured out. She asked, 'What will happen when you come up against the sharp edges of the institution?' I said that I didn't know, but in this new world I felt I was in I would allow myself to experience that when it happened and see what the experience was. It might well be one that surprised me. What I was clear about was that if it meant that I was unable to be alive in the situation then I would leave. But until that point came I felt that the right thing was for me to stay where I was and seek to live out my trust there. Some weeks later I came across a book called *The Dance of Change* by Michael Lindfield, a book that seemed to me to be full of wisdom about spiritual growth.[2] In it he emphasizes that the context in which to grow and be transformed is that of our

families, work, neighbours, where we are, not in dashing off
to join or (even worse) found communities.

Re-connecting with work and the institution has proved to
be a struggle. I came back from my travels with a clear picture
of some of the areas I wanted to work in, things I wanted to
create to make spaces for people whose longing to connect
with themselves, their lives, nature and God were not being
met by the institutional church. I have had the privilege of
creating some of those opportunities both within and outside
the context of my work, and have felt privileged and nurtured
and sustained myself in many of them. Others have met with
little response. The Bishop has agreed that spirituality should
be a focus of our work alongside the other things we hold
responsibility for. I have been frequently surprised by the
depth of encounters I have had, often with unexpected
people. People have commented on the way in which some of
the distance and aloofness they felt from me seems to have
been replaced with someone more gentle and approachable.

But so many other aspects have felt mundane, irksome,
unrewarding, pointless. Meetings which beforehand I would
have attended enthusiastically I found myself unwilling to
make the effort to go to. We have been through a time of
major transition in our team and I have found it difficult to
generate the energy to build the new team or to think through
the shape of the new courses we need to design. I was clear in
making the decision to return to working with the Diocese
that I was re-committing myself to that for a significant
period of time. And yet it has been difficult for my heart to be
in it. It feels as though my head has been in one place and my
heart in another, but quite whereabouts my heart is has
eluded me. Shortly after returning to work I went down with
a mysterious virus which knocked the stuffing out of me. For
the first time in my life I had to ring two groups where I was
due to lead sessions at the last moment to say, 'I can't come.

You'll have to carry on without me.' When I had rung the second and put the phone down, I burst into tears because I felt so bad at letting people down through physical weakness.

I had written an account of my travels and exploration into sacred space in liaison with a well-known religious publisher with a reputation for a broad outlook who had been very encouraging about the writing and the possibility of publishing the book and had seen the first chapter. It was with some confidence therefore that I sent off the completed manuscript having revised it in the light of comments from friends. I sensed that something was wrong when it seemed that the phone line went dead. I rang to find out what was happening and my editor was brief – the meeting to decide on the book was in a few days and I could find out after that. I rang her. They had decided to turn it down on the grounds that 'it wasn't Christian enough for their market' and they felt it was too 'new age'. It felt as though my worst fears had been realised, that the journeying had put me into a 'no man's land' acceptable neither to the Christian world, nor the secular.

The Christmas and New Year after my return to work in September seems to have been something of a watershed. I spent New Year's eve in bed with a violent tummy bug, retching painfully. Two days later I woke up and it was as though something had shifted inside me. I had started to grow a pony tail the previous year and I decided to have it cut off. It felt as though it symbolised a heart decision to be where I am, to live life to the full in my context, to be who I am in the midst of all the things which hold me to this place, this set of relationships, not to try to express something else. With the decision came a new release of energy. Winter has felt different, something to be welcomed rather than endured or escaped from. I don't know how things will be but I know that I am now back from my travels.

Connecting with masculinity

But there was still another piece of connecting to do, and this has also proved to be difficult. One area that I have toyed with, read about, thought of doing something about, is my identity as a man. I had always drawn back and been relieved when it didn't quite fit in to go on any 'men's workshops'. This was another area which I had in the back of my mind as something I wanted to take the risk of diving into, so when the opportunity of going on a men's weekend in the midst of nature came up on my travels I decided to go. I was encouraged by my experience of the dance at Findhorn, where I connected powerfully and emotionally with another man. I have always found the masculine side of myself difficult to accept. I am frightened of its anger, potential aggressiveness and power to hurt. I feel that my feminine side is more acceptable to me and others, with its gentleness and emotion. In the dance I had seen something of my beauty as man in both the aggressive power *and* the gentle intimacy. And, as someone pointed out, the beauty I had seen in the man I had danced with so intimately was a reflection of the beauty in myself as a man. And yet there are still many aspects of myself as a man which I find difficult to live with, so it was with a lot of fear that I set off. I don't enjoy being in the company of other men. I always feel somehow safer and more relaxed if women are present.

The workshop took place on the edge of the Lake District. We met in the car park at the bottom of a track, off a tiny country road that wound over the moors. Most of the others knew one another but were friendly to me. From the car park we had a mile-and-a-half trek through thick wooded country by a river, up and down narrow paths and across narrow, swinging bridges which threatened to throw us into the river at the slightest slip of the foot, to reach what felt like an island with the river on three sides and a steep hill on the other. Like some of the others I did the 'macho' thing of picking up too many bags of food to carry, cursing myself as the way got steeper and longer, but doggedly carrying on. We arrived at a 'camping barn', a two-storey stone building with water pumped out of the river. I was reassured to find even those who had been before helplessly milling around, trying to work out how to get the pump going, as one expectation of the male role I have never lived up to is being practical – Sirpa does the practical tasks around the house.

The focus for the work of the week was the fire. We met around an open fire, sitting in a circle, fifteen of us in all. I found it a moving, enriching and difficult experience. On the first morning it was clear that there was a lot of anger which people had brought with them. Our facilitator suggested that we clear a space around the fire, and in turn come up to it and speak our anger, or anything else we wanted to say, into it. In no time people were expressing deep-seated feelings of rage at parents who had died young, anger with work situations, anger about what men do to each other and to women with their anger in places like Bosnia. I had longed to connect with my father and had rung him after my last journey to find that he didn't seem to want to know what I had been experiencing. I roared the rage I felt. And somehow it was as though the fire was able to contain the rage, and we were able to hear and receive so much anger poured out.

Aspects of the experience were deeply affirming of my journey. I had written in my diary the previous week, 'There is no turning back.' At one point, three of us were sharing what was happening in our lives in a small group. When I had shared my recent experiences, one of the others said, 'It sounds as though for you, there's no turning back.' That evening we decided to go and search for a stone which expressed our situation at that moment, and come back and use it as a symbol to share with the group. I went off, found a stone which expressed the difficulty of relating to my father and brother, another which expressed how I felt within myself, and another which formed a base on which the two could stand. Then I decided to cross the river. There didn't seem to be a way across without building some stepping stones, which I saw as a possibility of another way of coming at the relationships. Then I suddenly spotted a route across and made my way over, balancing precariously on the stones. I worked my way along the other side, but gradually the path became a narrow ledge of stone above the river, with a cliff above me. Then the ledge of rock came to an end so that I was clinging to the cliff as the water rushed underneath . 'That's all right,' I thought, 'I can always go back the way I came.' I couldn't. I could not. I could not find any route back across the river! I had to climb the cliff to get back, but in doing so I came across some wild raspberries and took fifteen of them.

Back at the fire our facilitator suggested that we build a theatre stage and decorate it. He had paper bags and night lights. Each in turn told the story of their stone, put a night light on it and placed it in the bag. As darkness fell, more and more lanterns appeared as each told their story. When I had told mine, I passed the raspberries round and we ate them together as a thanksgiving for the sustenance the universe gives us. After all the stories had been told we opened some wine and shared it. It felt like a precious moment of communion with other men, with the nature around and with God.

I was struck by how spirituality had come to the fore for so many of the men in one way or another over the past few months. One had felt led out of the blue to go to a Quaker meeting and had joined the Quakers and started to pray. Another had felt drawn to go to a church, had had an overwhelming sense of Christ filling him, but when he had tried to share it felt patronised, and discovered that when he wanted to hear other people's experiences of Christ they quoted the Bible at him as though they were afraid of contact at a human level. Sadly, he had left the church, but was encouraged at meeting me, because he felt I was the first Christian he had met who understood something of his experience and that there must be a place in the Church where he could find sustenance.

The following morning was deeply moving as people shared in depth. Several cried as they shared. I saw a whole deep side of one man whom I had seen as very superficial. I took the plunge and shared aspects of my sexuality which I struggle with. Others shared some of the same struggles and I was encouraged by that, but I found that it touched a part of me that felt very blocked deep inside and that I was unable to reach beyond the block. I felt weak and shaky. On the way home I felt sick and vomited on the motorway hard shoulder. The next day I was ill with food poisoning, aware of connections between the illness and the blockage, but unsure what was to do with which. It is an area that I shall do more work on. I know that it was only the safety of the group of men committed to share in trust and love, and the container of the nature all around, and the experience of the fire as creating sacred space that enabled me to share what I did and that will be a painful part of my continuing journey.

It left me concerned about my relationship with my father and brother, my seeming inability to connect with them, my fear of them. For my birthday present Sirpa had given me a session in a 'flotation tank'. A flotation tank is an enclosed, small space, filled with warm, highly salted water. You lie in it in darkness and the water holds you so that you are able to relax totally. In its own way, it too feels like a type of sacred space, a womblike place where one can totally let go and be. As I lay there I felt strongly the desire to connect with the male members of my family, and imagined what I would write to them. I composed the letters in my mind, went home and wrote them, expressing my longing, but making it clear that the problem was mine and I was not expecting any particular response from them. Both of them responded, my brother phoning me, very accepting and understanding of what I had written, my father, writing, expounding his philosophy of life, but also reasons in his past for his difficulties in relating emotionally to anyone. And so, out of the experience, I feel as though new connections are being made, however fragile.

But what had I learnt about sacred space and sacred places? Were there any conclusions that I could draw?

Notes

1. *Just Spirituality in a World of Faiths*, B and T Butler, Mowbray 1996
2. *The Dance of Change: an eco-spiritual approach to transformation*, M Lindfield, Routledge and Kegan Paul 1986

9

Reflections on Sacred Space

And the end of all our exploring
Will be to arrive where we started
And know the place for the first time.
T S Eliot[1]

I saw a new heaven and a new earth, for the first
heaven and the first earth had vanished.
Revelation 21:1

A new way of seeing

My journey into 'sacred space' took me on to an edge – the edge between Christian and pagan, between the Church and nature, between Christian faith and other ways of experiencing the world. As I walked on the edge I found it was there that I experienced God in a new way, on the margins, at the boundary points. I found God precisely at the point where my fear that I would end up being in 'no man's land' had held me back from going. The God I discovered on the edge is the God who is love, whose universe is love, whom I can trust utterly for every moment of each day. I discovered the God who has given my soul possession and who nourishes and sustains me every second; the God whose love and presence is mediated to me in and through everything, everyone I meet, every event in my life, however good or bad.

215

Travelling into sacred space has given me new experiences and allowed me to see new possibilities, new ways of being. It is as though a filter was lifted from my eyes for a period, enabling me to see things more clearly and experience them more passionately. As I opened myself up to the journey both to exterior places and into my own interior life I have touched parts of myself that I had forgotten were there. It has given me a different perspective, a different frame through which to experience, evaluate and live life. There is a sense in which things are just the same and I am the same person. But in another sense they can never be the same again because I have experienced a different way of seeing. Things which before seemed so essential can never reassert themselves in the same way. And my life will always be denuded if others I have touched are not part of it. Having experienced what it is like to live out from the centre of who I am in the present moment, I am aware of how pale by comparison any other way of living has become.

More fundamentally it has raised the question, 'What is the real world?' People have said to me on my return, 'Well, you're back in the real world now.' But the 'real' world for me can no longer be the world I left some months earlier. It can only be that world *experienced in the light of the other worlds I have visited.* That other world has not only been the physical places visited but the world of sacred space. And that world has had a reality about it for me which places a question mark over the reality of the world I experienced before. One of the striking things about the Celts seems to have been their ability to live simultaneously with a sense of the reality of the sacred world, which they called 'the otherworld', alongside their sense of the reality of the material world and an ability to experience God manifested equally through both. Having discovered the power of the 'otherworld' I am aware of the temptation of seeing that as the real world; of experiencing the world of sacred space, sacred places, sacred experiences as being the only one which has meaning, and so spending my life trying to recreate them. Perhaps that was what I was trying to do before Christmas and why it was so hard to re-connect with the world I had left. At the same time it would be equally mistaken for me to see all that experience as being a fantasy, like a drug-induced 'trip', and conform to the worldview I left. The challenge, the new possibility for me, is to live in my current world in the light of the worlds of sacred space. And I am only just beginning to discover what that means.

As I begin to integrate the experience I am realising that the effect of entering sacred space is not to distance us from the ordinary but to make the ordinary itself special. On the island I became aware of the quality and sacredness of all things – the simplest food, the act of stepping on grass, the feel of the wind and the sun, the experience of being alive. It was something of that sense of the sacredness of the whole of life that enabled me to experience it in the ordination service, in the everyday aspects of life at home, in the meadow in Northumbria, in the relationships that I had taken for granted. Travelling into sacred space helps to heighten our awareness so that we can more readily see the sacred in the everyday.

However, experiencing those other worlds has meant that I have had to take risks, be prepared to let go of the maps and directions, to step like Abraham into the unknown, not knowing what would happen, how it would be, but trusting God. As long as we cling to the world as we know it, looking for things to reassure us that it is as we believe it to be, relying on our maps, always looking back to the past and never on to the future, we will never discover the multitude of worlds around us. Our experience of God will be constrained and limited, because the God who meets us through the pages of Scripture is the God who time and again leads his people out of safety and security into the unknown. It involves what Reuben Alves describes in these words: 'One must forget in order to remember, one must unlearn in order to learn anew'.[2] I am convinced that I was only able to experience some of the richness of the world of the sacred because I took the step of letting go, launching out. One of the most powerful images of the Celtic saints is what appears to be their willingness to launch out into the unknown, trusting the wind and the tides to bring them to where God wanted them to be.

I not only had to take the risk of letting go and leaving home. I also had to be open to whatever the experience of sacred places would bring. I had to be prepared not to pre-determine what I would discover, what might turn out to be of God. It would have been easy for me to have gone to Findhorn, for example, with very clear views of what I would discover, and to have come away with my pre-judgements confirmed. Had I done so I would not have experienced the things which I believe have deeply enriched my life and my understanding of God. That is different from going naïvely and uncritically. It meant for me constantly reflecting on the questions: 'What am I experiencing? What do I make of it? What is it saying to me? How do I evaluate it in the light of my understanding of Christian faith?' But I needed to do that as I opened myself to the experience, rather than allowing my mental questions to prevent me from entering into it.

As I did so I discovered that sacred space contains darkness as well as light. Some of the experiences faced me with pain as well as joy, bleakness as well as beauty, the shadow side as well as the open. It seems that the experience of sacred space would have been incomplete without that. Otherwise it would have been an experience of floating above the earth rather than one of finding myself more deeply rooted within it. Journeying into sacred space proved to be a journey into the reality which lies both at the heart of the universe and in my own being, in which both darkness and light are integrated in the love of God. I feel that through the journey I have begun to touch the way that journeying into the sacred involves integrating the shadow side of ourselves, and that I am at the beginning of a process which will occupy me for the rest of life.

My experience has also reinforced my feeling that once we embark on the journey we discover that it has no end. There are turning points, milestones, major steps. Sometimes we give time and attention to the journey, to making particular explorations. These may be internal ones through a period of seeking counselling or prolonged retreat or other ways of focusing on our interior life. They may take the form of external journeys, pilgrimages to particular places, travel to other lands. There is always the temptation of thinking that this will be the journey to end journeys; this is the one which will mean that I am sorted out, or my faith is sorted out, or my life is sorted out. But each part of the journey opens up new opportunities, new questions, new challenges as well as giving us new resources. I am aware that there will be new edges which God is calling me towards. Some of them will be frightening and it will feel easier to hold back. But just as I stood on the cliffs where my tent rested precariously on the overhang, and looked down and breathed into the fear and discovered that it was not unbearable, I believe that at every edge, every boundary, I will discover God already there. I can trust God to lead me and be God and that the God I discover will be love, is love and always has been love. If there was one thing more than any other that I feel I have brought back with me from the travel it is that sense that God can be trusted wherever our footsteps might lead us.

Sacred places

On the journey I had discovered that there are special, 'sacred' places which have a power of their own. What made them sacred seemed to be a combination of the expectations and feelings that I brought to them, together with something inherent in the places themselves, which shaped and sometimes transformed my experience of them. There is a lively debate that rages between those who say that there is nothing special about places themselves, it is only what we bring to them which makes them sacred for us, and those who say not only that places are sacred in and of themselves but we can be very precise through the study known as 'geomancy' about what makes them sacred, and so lay down rules for sacred space. My experience, borne out by those who responded to the questionnaire I produced, indicates that the truth lies somewhere between those two positions, in a subtle interaction between what people themselves bring to sacred places and what the place itself gives to them. So I experienced the power of places to change my mood. I also frequently experienced the power of places to creep up unawares, as it were, and tap me on the shoulder so that suddenly I would find myself in a sacred place totally unexpectedly. At the same time I discovered how my mood and the weather could affect my experience of places, and how my experience was shaped by what I had read and heard before visiting.

One of the things I had set out to do was to see if I could identify any key features which made certain places 'sacred' ones, rather than simply striking or aesthetically pleasing. As I travelled I collected evidence by describing everything I could see at each site into a dictaphone and then transferring the information on to a site report form. This enabled me to make comparisons between different sites to see if common characteristics recurred. I read as much as I could find about the history of sites and what other visitors had experienced at them. I also sent out a questionnaire to two hundred people, seventy-four of whom replied, which in questionnaire response terms is a very high proportion. Among other things I asked people whether there were places which for them operated as 'sacred places' and, if so, what they were and what made them 'sacred'.

At first I was disappointed that there did not seem to be even one feature that all the sites had in common that I could pinpoint as being *the* thing which made them 'sacred'. At the same time there were a number of features which seemed to repeat themselves. As I reflected on this it suddenly struck me that:

There are no essential or necessary factors which have to exist in order for a place to be recognised as a sacred place. However, there are a number of qualities or factors which one can look for, and any sacred place will have at least one, and probably a combination of some of them.

It is difficult to put qualities into words because they are attempts to describe experiences which by their nature seem to defy definition. Although analysis of this sort of data is necessarily subjective, the qualities which appeared to repeat themselves both in my experience of visiting sites and in the things people said in the questionnaires were:

1. A quality of unusualness which could be unusual or very striking geographical features (eg a prominent hill rising out of a large plain), the venue of an unusual event (eg a miraculous healing, a burning bush undamaged by fire, the appearance of the Virgin Mary), or association with an unusual person (eg someone who is recognised as having been a saint).

2. Life-giving features, particularly the presence of clear, unpolluted water such as that from a spring or well.

3. A combination of natural features which form some kind of harmonious relationship to one another.

4. A form of 'enclosure' which marks it off as sacred space. This could be a natural feature, a simple circle of stones, or a

sophisticated series of walls and entrances.

5. The effect of generating a deep level of renewal and energy in those who visit (significantly different from a cup of tea!).

6. The effect of generating a quality of quietness not ordinarily experienced.

7. A sense of a place visited respectfully or prayed in over time, which inculcates in visitors a desire to pray or worship.

8. The effect of generating in visitors a sense of mystery.

9. The effect of generating in visitors a sense of awe.

10. A simplicity of form and style using for example a harmonious relationship of circles and straight lines.

11. A balance of space and light so that the light is perceived as being appropriate to the space, combined with a harmony of scale so that the proportions 'work' and the space is not experienced as being too large or too cramped.

12. A quality of experience of nature that seems out of the ordinary.

13. The generation of a perception of a physical link between the earth and the sky.

14. The 'dome of the sky' being either physically visible or reflected in a dome-shaped structure.

15. A focus within a structure through a symbol of the 'holy' (eg an 'altar').

It seems to me that any place which has a number of these features is likely to be a 'sacred' place, and that any places which are recognised as being 'sacred' would have at least one of these features and probably several. At the same time, however, there still seems to be something mysteriously elusive about sacredness. Most books on sacred places do not attempt to define what they mean by 'sacred' and assume its meaning. Academic attempts to define it, like those of Rudolph Otto in the book *The Idea of the Holy*[3] or Mircea Eliade in *The Sacred and the Profane*[4] seem to raise as many questions as they answer. The most helpful working definition I came across on my travels was one given to me by Joan, whom I met at Findhorn. 'There are some places,' she said, 'which when you walk into them, you, the universe and God all seem to melt into one.' That seemed to express something of the sense of connectedness that I had had so often, a sense of time standing still and everything focusing down into a single entity of oneness. At times it felt like a mystical experience where for a moment I would be caught into another world where everything formed a single unity. But what struck me was that instead of losing my sense of who I am, I felt more wholly and completely my unique self than at any other time. It is as though in that mystical experience of sacredness two essentially different ways of being come together into one. There is no division between what is 'other', spiritual, of God, and what is 'here', material, of the senses. At the same time neither is swallowed up by the other.

The importance of place

And time and again the key to that happening for me was visiting particular places. This reflected my experience throughout my life, where particular places seemed to speak to me so powerfully that I could only conclude that I was experiencing God, but also reflects the experience of God's people recorded through the Bible. Throughout Scripture we find particular places like Sinai, Mount Horeb, Jerusalem, Galilee, and types of place like the desert or mountain tops playing a key role in people's experience of God's self-revelation, so that frequently people's experience of God was mediated to them through particular places. The Scriptures offer us this sense of God being especially present in and made known through particular places but hold that together with a sense of God who is not confined to any one place but who inhabits the heavens. This is a creative tension that we find reflected within every major religion. When we look at Christian traditions we can see some which emphasize God being present in people not in place, and others which emphasize God being present in particular holy places and rituals. The Christian Scriptures would suggest that both are important strands.

When I sent out the questionnaire I was unsure to what extent my experience of God's self-revelation through particular places would be shared by others. One of the striking things which emerged was the number of people who felt that place was central to their experience of God, and that the nature of the experience would have been fundamentally different had it happened in a different place. The questionnaire itself had clearly sparked something for many of those who replied, with people writing at great length and frequently passionately about particular places and how they had spoken to them of God.

Through my travelling and reading I had discovered just how central a sense of place was for the Celtic Christians. Could it be that in our increasingly mobile society, where we are losing a sense of rootedness, we are finding a need to rediscover the link between place and spirituality which is why we are experiencing a revival of interest in the Celtic tradition? Could it also be that the pendulum has tipped too far in the direction of God being present in people rather than place, and that we are experiencing the deep spiritual need for a sense of God in and through place reasserting itself? This appears to be happening not only in the sections of the Church where one might expect it, but also in the evangelical wing which has traditionally emphasized the personal nature of individual salvation and the people of God being where God dwells. We are currently seeing phenomena like the Marches for Jesus which are partly about 'claiming places for God' and which seem to be expressing an intimate connection between God and place.

In visiting such places I had discovered the importance of the ways we enter and leave sacred space. Many pilgrimage sites regulate the way in which pilgrims approach the sacred place through particular rituals carried out. The final approach to the top of Croagh Patrick was marked by the circling of the cairn of stones seven times at the first station. The change to a different interior space frequently came as I was making the approach to sacred places. They were often difficult to get to, involving crossing water or climbing a hill. Created sacred places like cathedrals almost always have an entrance which is low, dark and which slows the visitor down, preparing them for entering the interior. The same is true of leaving. There is something about the nature of sacred space which makes it difficult to rush out of them. By their nature they seem to slow the visitor down, and something of the place lingers with them as they go, affecting their experience of the life that they return to. It became important therefore not only to pay attention to what happened in the place itself but in the approach to it and the leaving of it.

God and nature

In visiting sacred places I had experienced the most powerful sense of God coming through nature, through the experience of feeling part of and one with the earth. I had powerful experiences of the earth as a living, animate being, charged with energy which had the power to refresh, renew and revitalise me. I had experienced that particularly through trees, and discovered the ways in which different types of tree give off different types of energy which seemed to resonate with different parts of my body. I had experienced particular natural places as touching a depth of emotion in me which at times led me to cry.

Through the questionnaire I had discovered that this was an experience shared by many churchgoing Christians. I knew from reading the results of research carried out by the Alister Hardy centre in Oxford and parallel research in America that when people are asked to describe religious experiences many of them talk about experiences in nature. I wondered what would be the case for churchgoers and expected that for most of them their experience of God would be through religious contexts. To my surprise, experiences of God through nature predominated, with some people stating specifically that they feel closer to God outside than in religious buildings or worship. This bore out my experience of leading workshops on Celtic spirituality in which people are encouraged to work with objects taken from nature, and to see nature as expressing God. Frequently people will come up and say something like, 'I've never spoken about this before but my deepest experience of God is when I am out in nature and particularly. . . .' They then go on to describe the powerful sense of God they have through specific natural phenomena.

To my surprise this sense of God in nature was more marked in those who had lived all their life in cities than it was for those who had lived in the country. I had expected that those who had lived in the country would be attuned to nature and would be more likely to identify natural places as sites of experiencing God. I had thought it might be less true for those living all their lives in cities, and was struck at how it was more the case for them. It seems that something of the rhythm of nature touches the most urban of people somewhere in the core of their being at a level beyond a romanticised, middle-class vision of idyllic rural life. I believe that there are huge implications in this not only for how we plan our cities so that they enable people to tap into nature's rhythms, but also for further exploration around how and where people can discover sacred space in the city.

The sacred and sexuality

I also discovered in exploring sacred places that the masculine and feminine aspects of myself were touched. It was as though an exploration of the sacred was incomplete without the two sides of myself being brought into focus, with the beginnings of an integration between them. When I was thinking about the exploration I went to see Lavinia Byrne, who at that time was the person in the national ecumenical movement responsible for encouraging the development of healthy relations between women and men in the churches and society. As I got up to leave I started glancing through her bookshelves which contained a number of books about 'the goddess'. I remember her picking one out and saying, 'In any exploration of sacred space you will encounter her.' At the time I had very mixed feelings of fascination combined with fear. There is a powerful stream of current writing which links sacred places and the concept of 'mother earth' with feminism. They argue that Christianity and the other major religions are inherently male-dominated in their theology and structures, and that what is needed is the recovery of the feminine at the heart of the universe. Many are involved in creating new rituals and recovering old ones to celebrate this feminine force, sometimes called 'the goddess'.

I found that because sacred space touched me so intimately it led me to engage with my sexuality at a new level. Through touching vulnerable places in myself it seemed to release feelings which felt as though they are part of my femininity. At the same time I found myself being put in touch with and

needing to explore my masculinity. I experienced the attractiveness of the goddess concept, with its sense of life-affirming
energy which is about releasing creativity not dominating and
controlling. I warmed to a movement which seeks to redress
the balance and do away with a dualism which splits the
world into two. On one side is the masculine which is linked
with the rational, logical, godly and is seen as being superior,
and on the other side is the feminine which is linked with the
irrational, emotional, material and anti-godly and treated as
being inferior. At the same time I felt deeply uneasy with
aspects of it which seemed to me to be replacing one hierar-
chy with another. In place of one in which the masculine is
central and normative is put another in which the feminine
becomes central and normative and the masculine negative.
The question I found myself wrestling with was that of
finding a place for my masculinity as well as my femininity,
and coming to terms with my male identity. The experience of
meeting with a group of men in a context where we could be
vulnerable with each other was one of finding a place for the
two aspects of my being to be present. There was room for
aggression and anger alongside gentleness and tears in a way
I found both healing and unsettling.

The sacred and 'paganism'

In all of my exploring I discovered that I could no longer put
things into neat boxes in which there was a pure Christianity
on one side and an ugly 'paganism' on the other. The experience of God on the island was one which seemed to run
deeper than those distinctions, and I met people whose beliefs
would be self-confessedly 'pagan' who conveyed more of God
to me than many Christians. The encounters with God
through the places I visited seemed to come through elements
which were as much 'pagan' as Christian. What was more,

my reading and reflection led me to the conclusion that this
has always been the case throughout the Judaeo-Christian
tradition. Reading the lives of the saints of the Celtic church
is like reading the lives of pagan wonder workers. The sense
of trinity was central to the pre-Christian Celtic religious
worldview, and at least one writer has suggested that it came
to find its centrality in the Christian tradition through that
route. Certainly the trinitarian prayers of the Celtic Christian
tradition have a very similar rhythm and feel to 'pagan' ones.
We find the same in other traditions. Recently I gave a group
copies of St Francis's canticle of creation in which he celeb-
rates 'brother Sun' and 'sister Moon' along with the elements
of earth, fire, water and air. A number of hymns that we sing
today have been based on this such as 'All creatures of our
God and King'. One woman picked it up and said in disgust,
'But this is "new age"!' This is another illustration of how
difficult it is to separate things out and say, 'This is OK but
this is not'.

For some Christians the Bible is what enables us to test
what is pure Christian and what is pagan. But what do we
make of Jacob raising his stone as a pillar and declaring it to
be the dwelling place of God (Genesis 28:18, 22), or Joshua
building a stone circle at Gilgal to celebrate the crossing of the
Jordan (Joshua 4:19, 20 – the name 'Gilgal' means 'circle'),
both of which became major centres of worship? Or what do
we make of the descriptions of Moses doing magic with sticks
turning into snakes in combat with Egyptian magicians
(Exodus 7:10–12), or Elijah calling down fire on a dead bull
to prove that his god is better than that of the surrounding
peoples (1 Kings 18:21–40)? What do we make of the fact
that Jesus's birth is foretold by astrologers, and of the way he
identified with those considered unclean and impure, publi-
cans and sinners, by eating with them? What do we make of
people being healed through Paul's handkerchiefs being

passed on for them to touch (Acts 19:12)? These are just a few examples which indicate that even within Scripture we cannot make hard and fast divisions and are always in an area where 'pagan' and 'Christian' are mixed. And it has frequently been pointed out that virtually every feature of present-day Christian worship has been borrowed from paganism.

Reflecting on my experience there seem to be two extremes. One is a starry-eyed acceptance of everything as being of and from God with no discernment of what may be unhelpful or dangerous. The other is an attempt to hold on to a 'pure' Christianity which tries to eradicate everything which might possibly smack of 'paganism', and taints many things which are inherently good as being 'new age', dangerous, to be avoided and condemned. One lacks discrimination; the other lacks trust. In making a journey deeper into God we need a fundamental trust in the one who has promised that the Holy Spirit will lead us into all truth, alongside a resolve not to pre-determine on the basis of our previous belief and experience what will or will not be capable of speaking to us of God. At the same time we need the wisdom of serpents to discern what is leading us away from the God of love who is at the heart of the universe and who, for Christians, is revealed in the person of Jesus Christ. We also need wise companions on the way to help us avoid self-deception.

Sacred events

I had also discovered that a journey into sacred space took me into sacred events as well as sacred places. Circle dance is often referred to as 'sacred' dance, and I experienced a number of the moments in dance as being sacred ones. I also experienced sacred moments in some of the sharing in groups, both at Findhorn and particularly on the men's weekend. I suspect that these other types of activity share some of the same characteristics as sacred places, such as the ability to generate an experience of deep stillness, mystery, awe and communion. It seems that there may be clues here for those seeking to create sacred space for others, whether that is in worship, group learning or engaging with creative arts.

The added factor in creating sacred events appears to be the use of ritual. Circle dance is very ritualistic in that a similar fundamental pattern is followed even when the themes are different in different groups with different leaders. A central focus including a candle is always present; there is a time of holding hands and being still at the beginning; the moment is 'held' at the end of each dance. Similarly a particular type of ritual is followed in many group meetings where the focus is in some way on the experience of the group. The effect is that often the group will experience 'sacred moments' where people have a sense of the magic and mystery of the group, and a silence will often fall which people will be reluctant to break. For me, those are moments when a sense of God seems to break through into the ordinary stuff of human inter-action.

Above everything else I had discovered that the created world is full of infinitely more richness and variety than I had imagined. It is all around us, but it takes time to see it. I had to stop what I was doing and give the time to looking, being, absorbing, allowing the created world to be present to me. At many points it felt that it would have been easier not to have bothered. Had I given in to that feeling I would have missed so much giftedness that lies in our beautiful, God-created world.

The experience of pilgrimage into sacred space is an intensely personal one. At times I wondered if I was being self-indulgent and engaging in something essentially indi-vidualistic, being caught up in the spirit of the age and caught up in the spirit of the age and avoiding dealing with the complex corporate issues which face our society. Should I not have used the time for exploring the relationship of Christian faith to issues of poverty or healthcare, for example? Through reflecting on the experience I became aware how impossible it is to disentangle what is individualistic and what is corporate. Sacred space itself has a corporate aspect. It is communities which recognise places as being sacred and use them as symbols which can help to give cohesiveness to a society. Some would argue that that is their primary function. I also discovered how important the personal is in motivating us to engage with the corporate in a different way. It enables us to be more in tune with the God of love at the heart of all things, instead of acting out of anger or bitterness or the need to justify our existence or the hundred-and-one screwed up motives with which we engage with issues. In this life we are unlikely ever to act out of pure motives. However, as we expose ourselves to the sacred it seems that we are enabled to grapple with the complex issues which face our society at a level and in a way which takes us closer to the heart of Jesus. The gospel writers present him as the one who not only brought the Kingdom of God but who expressed it in his own personhood.

Sacred space and the Church

I want to suggest some implications of this exploration for the institutional churches. Various writers have pointed out that we are in a period of major shift in culture and thinking, sometimes called a paradigm shift. One of the features of this period is the breakdown of the idea of universal ways of thinking and acting, and the recognition of value in diversity. Another is an emerging holistic consciousness in which everything is seen as being part of a wider whole, and in which the interdependence of all things, animate and inanimate, is becoming apparent. With this holism is coming the breaking down of the dualism between thinking and feeling, spirit and matter, mind and body, objective and subjective, masculine and feminine. There is a growing recognition that we need both the language of verifiable distinctions, the language of science and philosophy, and the language of symbol, metaphor and poetry. Neither is 'true' at the expense of the other. They are both necessary components of living in the complex universe of which we are a part. There is a recognition that the scientist uses intuition and imaginative leaps and sees things from the subjective viewpoint of the observer, and that at the heart of matter may lie not order and simplicity, but chaos and paradox. We are in an exciting, disturbing time when old distinctions and barriers are being broken down, and it is not clear what picture is emerging.

From a theological point of view this seems to be more true to how things have always been, with the Bible revealing God in and through periods of flux, change and development. At the heart of the writing of the early Christian thinkers lay an appreciation of the mysterious nature of God and the universe, with God as mystery being a predominant image. It seems that the idea of truth being a fixed, static, bounded thing, which can be clearly defined and used as a permanent criterion for judging everything, is a recent development which says more about a nineteenth-century worldview in which rational thought was believed to be capable of explaining and controlling everything than it does of the God revealed in Jesus Christ, and the development of God's people through the ages. As we listen to the perspective of Christians from other cultures, traditions and social situations, we are discovering how 'one-eyed' our understanding of the Christian faith has been. We are also learning that in some areas Christianity has contributed to destructive attitudes. For example, the idea of man having dominion over the created world has been mis-used to justify the exploitation of the environment, the cost of which we are only beginning to recognise.

My journey into sacred space took me into the world which expresses sharply some of the massive shifts taking place. From that perspective it seems to me that there is much for the Church to learn. One way of looking at the role of the Church is to say that it is a holder of sacred space for society. In other words, the Church should be what people turn to when they have a need to express their sense of that which lies outside them. Historically the Church has held that role, par-ticularly visible at the key rites of passage, when people have looked to the Church at times of birth, marriage and death, and in its role of consecrating particular buildings as sacred places. We now seem to be in a situation, however, where that is increasingly less the case, and we are seeing the rise of 'alternative' and 'secular' rites of passage to meet those needs, and where many 'consecrated' places are experienced as hav-ing less sacredness than many others. There are notable exceptions, as when the Liverpool church leaders led the sing-ing of 'You'll never walk alone' as part of an expression of the sense of the sacred following the Hillsborough football tragedy. In general, however, the Church appears to be in danger of losing that role of being a holder of sacred space in society and thus in danger of losing its role of bringing the good news of what God is doing in Jesus Christ to the world of which it is a part.

Theology and the living earth

The Church needs to develop its theology and practice in the light of the huge shift taking place in the understanding of the place of humanity in relation to the cosmos. We are becoming aware that far from being the focal point and pivot of the created order, we are one part of a delicate, finely balanced eco-system, which in its beauty and complexity reflects for the Christian the wonder of our creator God. We are also becoming aware of the precariousness of our continued existence on the planet because of the way we have abused it. In putting our focus on human beings and their needs at the expense of that of the environment we are in danger of destroying the very eco-system that sustains us and all life. The most conservative of estimates reckons that human beings are currently destroying natural species at thirty thousand times the rate that they would die out naturally. A number of Christian writers are beginning to look afresh at the Christian tradition from the perspective of what we now know about ecology, and inspiring new understandings of the tradition are beginning to emerge. A particularly powerful image which is emerging is that of the earth as our home. One thing which many people say when they come to an awareness of the earth as a living being is that they have a feeling of 'coming home'. Rather than being a 'conversion' it is a sense that they are rediscovering something which has always been within them from early childhood but which has lain dormant. And we seem to have become alienated from our 'home', the earth created by God which sustains our human existence, the earth which is 'the Lord's'. The fact that we are capable of unthinkingly covering our earth with litter was something which for me became a recurring symbol of that alienation from the earth and therefore from its creator God.

I am convinced that one of the key questions for Christian theology now is to understand the relationship of our tradition to the concept of the earth as a living, pulsating, animate being. I had experienced the earth in this way through my travels. This is a concept which is rapidly gaining popular support, sometimes referred to as the 'Gaia' hypothesis. In some of the forms in which it is emerging it is clearly at odds with major aspects of the Christian tradition, for example as we have seen in the link made with 'the goddess'. Other writers, such as the author of *The Celestine Prophecy*, are making a new religion out of the concept, and like the gnostic sects of early Christian centuries are claiming that they have the key to entering the new world which they describe as the 'nine insights'.[5] Sadly, because of these forms, many Christians refuse to have anything to do with explorations of God in nature and a recovering of a delight in the earth. They fear that any opening up in this area will put them on to a slippery slope leading to a watering down of the faith and a selling out to paganism and the 'new age'. They may be right, but I believe that they are wrong. I believe that enough diverse evidence is beginning to emerge for us to be able to say that there is something in this concept of the earth as a living being which has a ring of truth about it. The Hebrew people of the Old Testament appear to have had this understanding in calling on the whole creation to praise its creator. Rather than being afraid of this area, the Church needs to explore it. In the process I believe we will begin to recover fundamental aspects of our tradition and discover ways in which we have gone astray.

A few writers have recently begun to suggest that one way forward is to take a fresh look at our understanding of the Trinity. We have seen how this was a central element in the Celtic Christian tradition which enabled them to hold together a sense of an animate creation with biblical faith. It seems to me that we need to evolve a much more complex understanding of relationships in which nature is also seen as a partner. In this understanding the relationships are not only among people and between people and God, but also between people and nature and between God and nature. Nature therefore becomes an animate partner in the dynamic. The depth of the concept of threeness-in-oneness and oneness-in-threeness which the concept of the Trinity expresses is one which I believe can help us make sense of the complexity of that relatedness. Among other things, I believe that will involve a recovery of the importance of the wisdom literature in the Old Testament and Apocrypha, a tradition in which the created order plays an important role, one which Jesus drew on significantly but which has tended not to have had the attention which has been given to other aspects of Scripture.

Some very exciting work has begun along some of these lines, but unfortunately it has tended to be considered 'fringe' by church authorities, orthodox theology and many ordinary Christians. Sometimes this has been the fault of the writers themselves. For example, much of the creative work has been done by 'ecofeminist theologians', who in their attempt to forge new ways of looking at the tradition have invented new words. This sometimes makes them difficult to read, and alienates them from many who might warm to their message if they understood what was being said. It is also an area which needs to be approached on all sides with humility. People are too ready to create new maps, new orthodoxies in an area which by its very nature has a complexity. We need to approach this area wholeheartedly in terms of experience but cautiously in terms of explanation. If the earth is indeed a pulsating, living being, then it is an exceedingly complex one. We are barely at the beginning of understanding the complexity of the human personality and brain. If we, as humans, are one part of a living, interrelated, complex organism, then that organism itself is infinitely more complex than we can conceive. If that is the case then we are at the beginning of an exploration as exciting and significant as the initial exploration of the world and its geography. But we are only at the beginning. We need to be wary of assuming that we have found the maps which will describe it. It will only be as we continue to share our experi-

ences out of our very different starting points that I believe
we will be able to develop the maps we need. This will take
time, openness to dialogue and a refusal to take entrenched
positions.

Taking religious experience seriously

I believe that the churches urgently need to create a climate in
which people can freely talk about their spiritual experiences.
When David Hay of the Alister Hardy institute was researching religious experience, he discovered that the majority of
people interviewed had had deeply significant religious
experiences but that this was the first time they had talked
about them to anyone else.[6] We are now moving into a situation outside the Church where people are freer to talk about
spiritual experiences, as my weekend with the men's group
indicated. However, within the churches a taboo seems to
operate about speaking of experiences which do not appear
to fit in with the predominant 'orthodoxy' of the Church's
leaders. If, as seems to be the case, the majority of church
members have their most powerful experiences of God
through nature yet are hesitant about sharing those, and find
little opportunity for expressing that sense of God in Christian worship, it is hardly surprising that many are quietly
leaving the Church, and either slipping out of any community
expression of religious experience or occasionally finding
expression for it in fringe or 'new age' groups. I believe the
churches have a responsibility to take the religious experience
of their members seriously as part of the whole process of dis-
cerning God. This will involve creating a climate in which
such experiences can be shared, reflected on and related to
understandings of the Christian tradition, in an open atmosphere in which people will not be told 'You shouldn't be
believing or feeling or experiencing that'. There is nothing to

fear in doing that if we trust the Holy Spirit, who will lead God's people into all truth. I fear that if the Church goes on not taking people's experience seriously the current drift away of members will continue, and many may drift into neo-paganism where they will find opportunities to share their experience of God in nature and will encounter rituals designed to give expression to that.

Sacred worship

There are implications from the exploration for the churches' worship. At one time it would appear that the links between the Christian festivals and the celebration of the natural cycle of the year were much clearer. As with so much of our link with the earth, that connection seems to have been largely lost. As people re-connect with a sense of the earth being their home, and with a sense of the rhythm of nature, I believe that they will look for a celebration of that within their worship. If that is not found within the Church, many will look elsewhere.

It seems to me also that there are implications for worship in the qualities I have indicated which seem to generate in people a sense of the 'sacred'. One is that of generating a quality of silence. Most institutional church services have very little room for silence, and few clergy seem to have any idea of how to help a congregation enter into the experience of it. All too often there will be a token, 'We'll just have a moment of quiet,' during which there is just time for people to stop shuffling when the words take over and the service moves on. It may not be surprising that more and more people are turning to forms of meditation rather than to church worship for their communion with God. In all the furore which surrounded the news of the abuses generated by the leadership of the 'Nine o'clock' service which came to light during my sabbatical, I was struck by a comment of the Archdeacon of Sheffield that at least it had been a place where during the meditative part of the service he had been able to experience a depth of stillness within Anglican worship. Peter Stanford, commenting in the *Sunday Times* on the increasing number of alternative prayer books for non-churchgoers, describes those seeking new ways of praying as feeling 'alienated, or worse, assaulted by the all-singing, all-speaking, all-action services on offer in their local parish churches'.[7] I believe those responsible for leading worship should also be looking at the other qualities of sacred space, such as the generation of an experience of awe and mystery, alongside the importance of simplicity.

Another implication is the need for the Church to be the focus of unity of a diversity of expressions of spirituality, rather than trying to hold on to a token uniformity. I was struck in my travels by the increasing diversification which is happening in spirituality as much as in other areas. Much of the earth mysteries and related movements is very eclectic, taking bits from different places and different cultures. Much of it is small-scale with small groups of people bonding together around a common interest and expression, loosely affiliated to others through a series of networks, but each having its own autonomy. There are clearly strengths and weaknesses with this. The strength is that it enables every member to feel they have a stake in what is done and how it is done. It means that people can find expressions which are appropriate to them, rather than feeling that they have to conform to an alien culture in order to belong. The weakness is that groups can go down blind alleys, can engage in mutual self-deception, can reinforce their own views by never interacting with people of differing views. If manipulative figures are allowed to emerge as gurus such groupings can become places of abuse.

But whatever the weaknesses it seems to be the direction that society is taking, and to be likely to be a dominant trend at least well into the new millennium. As it develops, I believe more and more people within the church will be looking for the same diversity, variety and small-scale opportunity for expression of spirituality, whether that is expressed in Ignatian, Franciscan, contemplative, Celtic or other forms. It would appear that this role of holding together diversity of local expression may have been more the pattern of parts of the 'Celtic church' and may be another reason for its attractiveness to Christians today. It seems to me that the institutional church needs to be prepared to create and allow opportunities for such diversity to operate within the context of a framework of shared underlying belief.

Alongside the public, shared worship, I believe the Church should be encouraging the development of a variety of smaller groupings. These would include small meditation groups, groups exploring particular spiritualities, groups exploring nature and God. The common elements between such groupings would be a broad commonality of belief rather than of practice or expression. There would be occasions in which groups would come together to affirm their unity within diversity. In the major denominations this would focus around the sharing of the bread and wine, where all are 'one body' because all 'partake of the one bread'. This central coming together which would happen less frequently would be the focus of unity rather than of uniformity. Within the worship there would be a celebration of a variety of expressions of spirituality which would be given room. The message would be, 'Isn't it wonderful that within this diversity of expression we have this underlying unity in Christ which we can celebrate?' Many churches are seeing signs of diversity, with perhaps a quiet early morning communion, a mid-morning family communion and an evening youth service.

Sadly, however, none of them acts as a focus for unity, and the diversity is seen as being something to be regretted rather than celebrated. Other churches, notably some of the more fundamentalist house churches, are insisting on a greater uniformity of belief and practice. They are proving very popular, which is not surprising given the unsettling nature of the shift our culture is experiencing, but are in danger of ending up as fragile heaps of sand when the tide moves out, to be washed away when it returns. Nationally the churches are exploring what Christian unity means and how there can be unity in which diversity is not lost. However, unless that practice of encouraging increasing diversity at local church level is developed, it is in danger of becoming an exercise carried out by fewer and fewer people.

The sting in the tail for the churches is that allowing increasing diversity means church leaders, bishops and clergy letting go of power and control. It means being prepared to trust people and trust the Holy Spirit. It means being prepared to let go of pre-packaged beliefs and boundaries. It means being prepared to live with messy edges. It means not knowing everything that goes on and not being able to control what happens. Theologically, I believe it means clergy becoming priests rather than managers, and would be a process of liberation for church leaders as much as for church members. Understandably it seems that many of the churches are moving in the opposite direction and are trying to stop the tide of change by becoming more authoritarian. I fear, however, that unless a process of decentralisation and encouragement of diversity of spiritual expression takes place, the institutional churches will gradually and quietly die out. If that happens their historic role of being a holder of sacred space in the community will go elsewhere.

Notes

1. *Collected Poems 1909–1962*, T S Eliot, Faber and Faber 1963, p222
2. *The Poet, The Warrior, The Prophet*, R A Alves, SCM 1990, p18
3. *The Idea of the Holy*, R Otto, OUP 1950
4. *The Sacred and Profane – the nature of Religion*, M Eliade, Harcourt, Brace and Co 1959
5. *The Celestine Prophecy*, J Redfield, Bantam 1994
6. *Religious Experience Today*, D Hay, Mowbray 1990
7. 'Praying for a more spiritual change', P Standford in *Sunday Times* 27th Jan 1996

10

Invitation to Pilgrimage

Life everlasting
Love has prepared
The paths of your coming.
Kathleen Raine[1]

A door stood open in heaven and the voice that I
had first heard speaking to me like a trumpet said,
'Come up here . . .'
Revelation 4:1

We are witnessing a revival of pilgrimage in our culture. Because of that it has become the subject of academic interest with a lively debate about its meaning. Some understand it as a journey to encounter the sacred, that which lies outside ourselves. They point to the way pilgrimage is a feature of every culture and every major religion. Others see it as purely fulfilling social and cultural needs. They point to the way pilgrimage centres like Jerusalem have become the focus of conflict of different understandings of the meaning of pilgrimage, as an indication that pilgrimage is what we make it, not something in and of itself. Others take the middle ground and argue that going on pilgrimage is like entering into a landscape. We can take a variety of routes through any piece of landscape, but the nature of the terrain limits our choices and shapes the way

we travel. I found this a helpful image for what I had experienced in making a pilgrimage into sacred space. The other
explanation I found helpful is that what lies at the heart of
any pilgrimage is the stepping out of the ordinary structure of
our lives into a world of 'anti-structure'. We let go of the
things which give boundaries to our lives in order to enter
another world where we don't know our way around. It is the
experience of stepping outside our everyday life which
enables us to see things differently and to re-evaluate our
lives. And it is that stepping outside which allows us to open
ourselves up to being encountered by God in new ways.

This book is an invitation to pilgrimage, to step aside. It
may be only for an afternoon, an evening or a day. It may be
for longer. It may involve journeying to other countries, distant lands. It may only mean travelling a few yards. It may
focus on the exterior journey to other places or it may focus
on the interior journey within. But whatever the scope and
the scale of the venture it will have certain elements. It will
involve a stepping aside from the everyday. It will involve a
letting go. It will involve a deliberate act of opening oneself to
being encountered by the 'other'. It will involve making time.
It will involve a parting from home and a returning to home.
You may be wondering, 'How do I go about it?' What
follows are some suggestions from my own experience. As
you read them, you need to relate them to your circumstances
and personality. We are all different, and what works for one
person will not necessarily work for another. These are things
which I found helpful.

Find the trigger

There is a world of difference between saying to oneself, 'I
would love to go on pilgrimage, or visit X one day' and 'I am
going on pilgrimage' or 'I am going to visit X'. The first is a

wish; the second is a decision. For a wish to become a decision there needs to be a trigger. I vividly remember the trigger
which got me to the Celtic island of Iona. I had wanted to go
for many years and had frequently said to myself, 'One day I
would love to go to Iona'. Through a Creative Bible Study
network I convene I started to correspond with Giles David, a
member of the community on Iona. One day I had a letter
from him with the phrase, 'Today a whale swam up through
the sound.' The phrase leapt out at me and I decided that I
was going to that place. I did not expect to see a whale but
something in those words acted as a trigger which shifted me
from 'Maybe' to 'will'. It may be that for you this book will
act as the trigger. It may be something you see or hear. It may
be a crisis of some sort. What you need to do is to be open to
the trigger, recognise it when it comes, and respond.

Create the opportunity

If the trigger provides the motivation and comes from outside, the creating of the opportunity is something you have to
do. Any pilgrimage involves time and commitment. We have
to make the space and find a way. There are many ways of
doing that. Once I had made the decision to go to Iona, I
decided that a way of getting there, a way of creating the
opportunity, would be to make it part of my work by leading
a group there. That became my opportunity, but it was something I had to do. It involved clearing other space in my diary
and making a commitment to it. It involved taking the risk
that I might not be able to find enough other people wanting
to go to make it worthwhile. I was fortunate to be in a posi-
tion where I could do that, but even so it involved a lot of
hard work and some negotiation with colleagues and family.
The sabbatical journey into sacred space involved clearing a
major block of time. I kept putting it off because there was

always good reason not to go now. Either there was a major project getting under way, or there was a team member starting, or a team member leaving, or there were things needing attention at home. I quickly realised that there was a danger of never going, and so I had to decide a time in consultation with others involved and make other things happen around that.

Part of creating the opportunity is gaining an idea of where you want to go. The trigger will be the clue to that – what was it about it that acted as a draw for you? Was it to do with nature, travel, a particular sacred place, or types of sacred places? Was it stones and stone circles or abbeys or islands or holy wells or mountains? Was it a particular area? For me the area was the British Isles, and the draw was the challenge of visiting a variety of types of sacred place to see if they had common features. I then had to focus down on to particular areas. The choice of which areas to visit came out of reading about places and seeing which struck a chord with me, as well as talking to people about places which had moved them. Then there was a process of selecting, balancing time and budget, seeing what was possible and what would fit. Finally there was an element of 'happenchance', of keeping my eyes and ears open, of happening to see the brochure for Orkney and feeling my heart leap as I read it, of the midsummer festival at Findhorn fitting with the timing of visiting the island and with my budget.

Finding guides

Once you have created an opportunity I suggest that you find guides, both in terms of companions and books. Any pilgrimage will involve setbacks and difficulties. There are likely to be times when you feel that the possible outcomes are not worth the demands, and how much easier it would be to stay in your situation and not attempt to move out of it in any way. It is at those points particularly that one needs the encouragement of other people who understand something of what is involved. It is also helpful to have the advice and wisdom of people who have made a similar journey to the one you are making. My sense of despair in the early stages of planning my journey began to turn at the point where I met with Sister June and Brother Ramon, who encouraged me on the journey. You may be fortunate and know people who can act in that way for you. If not, then I suggest that you put out feelers. Ask people if they happen to know anyone who might be able to advise you. Keep your eyes and ears open in things you see and read for possible guides. Don't be afraid of taking the step of writing to someone. Those who have experienced the benefit of pilgrimage will generally be ready to encourage others to share the experience.

You may also want to find companions for the journey, to travel with you. My own preference is for solitude, and so I chose to make the journey alone. For other people, having companions is an important way of processing what they are seeing and experiencing – they make sense of things as they talk them out, not in silently reflecting on their own. If you are looking for companions I suggest that you don't necessarily think of the people that you know well and would be with in other situations. If one of the benefits of pilgrimage is stepping outside your ordinary world then doing that with people you know less well is part of the experience. If you are with people who are very much part of the pattern of your everyday life, you may not be able to let go enough to be open to the different experience into which you are travelling.

You will need books and maps and these will vary depending on what you are wanting to explore. Now that pilgrimage is becoming more popular there are guides to many particular places. For following in the footsteps of Ninian I used *A Way* to *Whithorn* by Andrew Patterson published by St Andrew Press (1993) which is excellent on the historical background but not so easy to follow on the ground. For following Cuthbert I used *Celtic Journeys in Scotland and the North of England* by Shirley Toulson published by Fount (1995). This put me on to various sites I would not have discovered otherwise, but the descriptions of how to find places were frequently unhelpful. I also used *Fire of the North* by David Adam published by SPCK (1993), which is an illustrated life of Cuthbert. A key map which I found indispensable for identifying sites and planning areas was the *Ordnance Survey Historical Map and Guide to Ancient Britain* which has the location of sites from earliest times to about AD 1000, colour coded and described so you know what sort of site it is. The map includes ancient barrows, standing stones and stone circles, castles, Roman remains, abbeys and churches among many others.

The best guide to stone circles I found is that by Aubrey Burl published by Yale University Press (1995) which is a paperback crammed full of detailed descriptions of circles and how to get to them. Particularly useful is its 1–5 grading, so you know how much there is to see at any site. I also used a book called *Prehistoric England* by Richard Cavendish published by Artus Books (1983). There are various guides written by Janet and Colin Bord. Two particularly useful ones are *A Guide to Ancient Sites in Britain* published by HarperCollins (1991) and *Sacred Waters* published by Granada (1983), which lists holy wells and springs. With all the guides, including the Ordnance Survey Historical Map, I found that local maps combined with a good road atlas were necessary to avoid missing places, or spending hours driving around trying to locate them. On Orkney I found the local guide book produced by the Tourist Office to be excellent.

Travel light

Once you have decided where you are going and have some idea of how you are going to get there you need to decide what to take with you. If, like me, you like your creature comforts, the temptation is to take enough of your 'home' with you to insulate you from the rigours of travel. My experience was that the lighter I travelled, the more free I felt to engage with the spaces into which I moved. Most of the time I camped, and I found that I needed very few clothes, for example. The key was to have flexibility of layers so that I could protect myself from the cold and rain where necessary, and still be comfortable if it became hot. The more I travelled the more I realised how little I actually need to live a fulfilled, rich, rewarding life. The joy of being in nature more than compensated for the lack of electricity and television. The fresh water from the well on the island was wonderfully refreshing in a way that our chemicalised tap water is not. All the things I thought I needed and would miss desperately became unimportant. When I was on my own I found that I ate when my body needed to eat rather than when my mind decided it was a meal time, and I discovered that I needed far less food that I eat normally. I lost weight and felt fitter and healthier and had more energy than I have for years. The lighter I travelled the better I felt and the more I enjoyed the experience. I still surrounded myself with books, many of which I never read because nature became my library, and I regret taking so many. I know that it would be easy to romanticise a simple life style, and that to live in that way permanently is very different from doing it temporarily with a warm, comfortable home to return to at the end of the travelling. But I encourage you to travel as light as possible. I believe that the clutter we surround ourselves with clutters our minds and spirits as well as our physical space. Preparing ourselves to enter sacred space involves stripping ourselves of physical as well as mental clutter.

Leave space

I am the sort of person who likes to have my life mapped out. I tend to fill my diary and my life with engagements, meetings, courses. I start planning holidays months in advance and work out all the things we can do and places we can visit while we are in an area. In planning this journey I chose to fight this preference and deliberately left parts unplanned with built-in 'maybes'. Some parts were planned and fixed in advance, like the weekend at Ammerdown, the arrangement with the fisherman to take me out to the island, the week at Findhorn, the pilgrimage up Croagh Patrick, but other parts were left open. Perhaps I'll go there for these few days or somewhere else. It was important to allow time for making detours, for new discoveries, for allowing one place to lead me on to another. It was important to have time for encounters with people and other pilgrims. A key part of the pilgrimage experience is the unexpected encounters and unexpected places that we discover along the way. If we cram our schedule too full we will miss them.

Go openly

We embark on pilgrimage because we have certain hopes and expectations. We may not be as clear as those who set out on the quest for the Holy Grail as to what we may discover, but we are likely to have some idea of what we are looking for. I discovered that a key to making pilgrimage was to be open to being encountered by God in ways I did not expect. Pilgrimage is about leaving our ordinary routine for a time and stepping into an unknown world. If we go with very clear expectations of what we will find, and end up only discovering and confirming what we already knew, then we will deny ourselves all that the journey may have to offer us. We need the spirit of the original explorers of our earth, setting out into the unknown, trusting God to lead us, open to the unexpected and new discoveries. Embarking on pilgrimage is to take a risk. It is a dangerous business. The risks may not be those of bandits, long distances and inhospitable desert areas which faced the mediaeval pilgrims. They are more likely to be risks that our assumptions about God, about life, about how things are, will be turned upside down. But my experience confirmed the gut feeling I had before that life without risk is not life worth living. It is certainly not the life that the God revealed in Jesus Christ calls us into. Whoever we are, pilgrimage can deeply enrich and transform our lives. Irenaeus, writing in the third century, wrote that the glory of God is a human being fully alive. Invitation to pilgrimage is an invitation to live life to the full.

Note

1. *Selected Poems*, K Raine, Golgonooza Press 1988, p45